Praise for

Biting the Wax Tadpole

"A tour of all the quirk and queerness to be found among the world's many dialects . . .
Little's meandering, highly-readable riffs on Finnish prepositions and
Incan counting systems manage to be funny and earnest—something of a feat for a book that
could be used as a grammar primer." —*The Onion's A.V. Club*

"A wrap-worthy language book." —*Boston Globe*

"It's clear that Elizabeth Little's omnivorous curiosity has suited her well . . . This short,
neon-colored book walks readers through categories that on paper should seem dry, from
pronouns to numbers, spicing everything up with cultural comparisons." —*Newark Star-Ledger*

"A surprisingly funny debut book." —*Boston Phoenix*

"*Biting the Wax Tadpole* is witty, sassy, and laugh-out-loud funny. Little convincingly
demonstrates that, as she puts it, 'language is nothing less than a great adventure.' So is her book."
—Kitty Burns Florey, author of *Sister Bernadette's Barking Dog*

"If you like language, you'll love *Biting the Wax Tadpole*. Elizabeth Little has mused on,
used, and even misused many of the planet's languages, and this fascinating
and often hilarious book gives a full account of her adventures."
—Ben Greenman, author of *A Circle is a Balloon and Compass Both* and *Superbad*

"*Biting the Wax Tadpole* is nothing short of fascinating. In a funny, friendly style, Little dishes
on everything you ever wanted to know about foreign language but were afraid it would take an
entire lifetime to find out." —June Casagrande, author of *Grammar Snobs Are Great Big Meanies*

SPI
EGE
L&G
RAU

BITING THE WAX TADPOLE

Confessions of a Language Fanatic

Elizabeth Little

Spiegel & Grau
NEW YORK
2008

Copyright © 2007 by Elizabeth Little

Published in the United States by Spiegel & Grau,
an imprint of The Doubleday Publishing Group,
a division of Random House, Inc., New York.
www.spiegelandgrau.com

A hardcover edition of this book was originally published
in 2007 by Melville House Publishing. It is here reprinted
by arrangement with Melville House Publishing.

SPIEGEL & GRAU is a trademark of Random House, Inc.

Book design by Blair and Hayes
Illustrations by Ayumi Piland, apakstudio.com

Library of Congress Cataloging-in-Publication Data
Little, Elizabeth.
Biting the wax tadpole : confessions of a language fanatic/
Elizabeth Little. — 1st pbk. ed.
     p. cm.
1. Language and languages. I. Title.
P107.L576 2008
400 — dc22
               2008012180

ISBN 978-0-385-52774-3

PRINTED IN THE UNITED STATES OF AMERICA

10 9 8 7 6 5 4 3 2 1

First Paperback Edition

For my mother

BITING THE WAX TADPOLE

Confessions of a Language Fanatic

INTRODUCTION

In the summer of 2000, I was in Nanchang, a fairly large city in southeast China that isn't exactly what I'd call a popular tourist destination. I'd spent the day on the road, stuck in the back of a sweltering bus that had broken down not once, but twice, and I hadn't eaten anything all day but some stale Chips Ahoy cookies I'd found in the bottom of my backpack. I was tired and cranky in the way that only those afflicted with bad luck and low blood sugar can be.

By the time I got into town, I wanted one thing, and one thing only: a plate of dumplings the size of my head.

As soon as I got off the bus, I dropped my pack at a hotel and went to the first restaurant I saw. I knew from experience that it was pointless to try to decipher a Chinese menu in my exhausted state, so I swallowed my pride, went up to the hostess, and very politely asked for an English menu.

"Nǐ yǒu méiyǒu yīngwén de càidān?"

The hostess responded with an expression that, sadly, I knew all too well: she had no idea what I was trying to say.

And I knew exactly what the problem was.

When you begin a course in Mandarin, one of the first things you learn is that the meaning of any given sound changes depending on your tone. Anyone with a mother is, of course, familiar with the linguistic peril of tone, but different languages use tone differently. In English, tone—or, more properly, intonation— usually applies to an entire thought: we pitch our voices up at the end of a question or we use mono- tone to convey sarcasm. In Chinese, however, tone can change the meaning of the words themselves. A single syllable—*ma,* to use the standard example— can mean mother, hemp, horse, or scold, depending

Pitch Problems

Underestimating the importance of tone in Chinese is easy when faced with an example like *ma*. I mean, what's the worst that can happen, right? Someone thinks that you're talking about hemp when you mean to be talking about a horse? At the very worst, it provides a bit of plausible deniability in the event of a run-in with local narcotics officials. Other words aren't quite so harmless, though. Take the sound *cao*. *Cao* shows up all over the place in non-threatening Chinese compounds like cottage, prairie, and lawn—in the third tone, the low dipping tone, *cǎo* can mean grass. But be careful, because in the fourth tone, the falling tone, *cào* means something very different: to fuck.

on whether the tone of the word holds steady, rises, dips, or falls.

When I got to China, I discovered that the first tone, the hold-steady tone, gave me all kinds of trouble. To really nail it, you have to speak it much higher than you expect, until you almost feel like you're singing the word. Unfortunately, singing isn't exactly my forte: the higher register of my voice can kindly be called "shrill." So every time I had to say a word with that troublesome high hold-steady tone, I would hold back a bit and try to get away with a nice, non-offensive contralto.

Which meant that every time I tried to say something with this first tone—in particular, the "dān" of càidān—I got it awesomely wrong. Like, first-round-of-*American Idol* wrong. So it wasn't at all surprising that the nice woman at the hostess podium had no idea what I was saying.

It had been happening for over a month at that point.

Before I traveled to China, I'd studied Mandarin for a year—two hours a day, five days a week—and I'd thought I was well prepared. I knew how to ask directions to a train station, bus stop, or Internet café. I was ready to yell at cab drivers and politely decline souvenirs, solicitations, and marriage proposals. But once I got there, my brain was fogged full of semi-familiar words and phrases, riddled with grammatical minutiae. Nothing came out the way I intended it to. My speech was an explosive mess.

I'd somehow managed to keep my spirits up for nearly a month as I blustered about, more often than not resorting to pantomime and occasionally to outright bribery to get a point across. I'd bungled conversations with government agencies, underground religious groups, and small children who were convinced I was some kind of monster, but until I got to Nanchang, I'd managed to keep my optimism intact, usually by reminding myself that I would never have to see these witnesses to my linguistic humiliation again. But that nameless, menuless eatery finally did me in. I was willing to admit defeat: I was total crap at Chinese. Not for the first time, I felt the bone-deep weariness of being a stranger in a strange-language land.

But I'd come this far, so I made one last, desperate effort—"càiDĀN!"—pitching my voice so high on the last syllable that I sounded like I'd been punched in the stomach.

A silence fell over the restaurant. The hostess furrowed her brow, the diners exchanged puzzled glances over their plates, and I resigned myself to yet another night alone in my hotel room, dining on chocolate chips and failure. But then, out of nowhere, a waitress in the back yelled "Càidān! Zhèige hěn dà de wàiguórén yào yīgè càidān!"

The huge foreigner wants a menu. I was so pleased I'd been understood, I almost forgot to blush.

•   •   •

Those of us in possession of the wallflower gene know that the world is full of special hells: communal showers; mandatory company parties; high school. And then there's travel. Travel's tricky, because unlike, say, high school, it can actually be simultaneously enjoyable and enlightening. But learning to speak a new language and engage with a new culture is a veritable minefield of potential misunderstandings and compromising situations. When you travel, you're not just paying for the privilege of seeing and experiencing new things, but also for the opportunity to make an ass of yourself.

Fortunately, there's another way. You don't have to jam yourself into a coach-class seat and sweat over itineraries and etiquette to get to know the languages and cultures of the world. Nor do you have to have a healthy trust fund or a perfect credit score. All you have to do is let go of those traumatic memories of mind-numbing middle-school Spanish class. Because once you're out of school, freed from the shackles of prescriptive grammar and college admissions requirements, the burden of language study gives way to the singular pleasures of language exploration— and the chance to discover the stunning diversity of human language and culture without even leaving the comfort of your own home. World travel isn't an option for everyone; word travel, on the other hand, is.

I think it's fair to say that I don't pick up languages. If anything, I roll around in them gracelessly and pray that something sticks. I speak halting Italian, and I rarely use French except as a way to swear at other drivers without fear of reprisal. I've stopped telling people that I studied Chinese because I'm sick of having to concoct plausible translations when asked to decipher calligraphy. Once I put Ancient Greek on my résumé. In high school. When I was applying for a job at Blockbuster Video. And then spent a summer being mercilessly teased for it. ("Thank god you're here, Elizabeth—we always wondered what we'd do if Plato applied for a membership.") Ever since, I've really tried to avoid the subject of Ancient Greek altogether.

Even so, languages are, without question, the great compulsion of my life.

My introduction to foreign languages came courtesy of my father, who, being a dutiful Canadian, felt it necessary to teach me a few key words in French. As such, I learned to say my name, to count, and to properly pronounce "Jean Béliveau." Much to my dismay, however, my study proved to be of little practical use. (St. Louis doesn't exactly have a thriving Francophone community.) Even when I did get the opportunity to practice my French on a family vacation to Europe, I was shockingly unable to strike up a single conversation about my name or knowledge of ice-hockey history. My taste for linguistic impracticality didn't get me into any real trouble until the fourth grade, when my elementary school decided—for reasons I suspect had less to do with staff qualifications than uppity parental demands—to start teaching us Latin. For the most part, class consisted of reviewing fancy Latinate vocabulary and learning about vomitoria. We did, however, get the occasional actual Latin grammar lesson, and it was during one

Famous Polyglots

Conventional wisdom would have us believe that we're either "language people" or we're not. I maintain that this is in large part codswallop: if you can learn a first language, you can learn a second one. But there's no denying that some people take to language like Rain Man takes to toothpicks. They don't need to learn languages, they

of these lessons that my latent love of languages truly came into view.

We were learning, appropriately enough, the conjugation of the verb "to love": *amare*. To the tune of the Mexican Hat Dance.

I'd never conjugated a verb before—not formally, in any case—and it triggered something deep in some anal-retentive cortex of my brain. After years of adopting and discarding a series of halfhearted hobbies (bugs, dinosaurs, ghostbusting), I'd found my focus. It helped that I always enjoyed learning

---

"pick them up," as if a new language were nothing more than an extra carton of milk from the grocery store. Take Anthony Burgess, for instance. When not writing masterworks like *A Clockwork Orange* or Rae Dawn Chong's dialogue in *Quest for Fire*, he managed to pick up eight languages fluently and gain familiarity with an additional five. James Joyce reportedly knew English, French, Spanish, Italian, German, Danish, Norwegian, Russian, Latin, Ancient Greek, Dutch, Slovenian, Croatian, Irish, and whatever it is that makes up *Finnegans Wake*. When she wasn't busy throwing an eye-pleasing wrench into the Roman political machine, Cleopatra was quite the accomplished linguist. Plutarch wrote that she "spoke most languages," which, at the time, meant at least the languages of Egypt, Ethiopia, Arabia, Syria, and Persia—in addition to her assuredly intimate grasp of Latin. But these linguistic feats positively pale in comparison to those of Francis Sommer, a German who reportedly picked up all the languages of Europe while on a trip to Russia. By the time he died in 1978, he was fluent in a truly mind-boggling ninety-four languages.

things by rote—and languages offered a nearly unlimited supply of potential memorization. But, more important, I loved a good mystery. My heroes were Harriet the Spy, Hercule Poirot, the entire cast of *Clue*. And a foreign language is like a mystery, a code to be cracked, a secret I could share in.

In other words, I was done for.

I made lists of languages that I wanted to learn by the time I was fifteen, twenty, twenty-five (the most distant age I could imagine at the time). I dreamt of keeping multilingual diaries so as to confound even the cleverest snoops. I made up my own languages, which I practiced on my cats.

Shortly thereafter, I purchased my first foreign-language dictionary, a slim volume of German and English that I ordered by mail. When it was delivered, my mother said to me, quite reasonably I think, "Just what do you think you're going to do with that?"

"Learn German," I said.

"But why?" she asked.

I shrugged. "Why not?"

•   •   •

The German dictionary was only the beginning. Fifteen years later, my apartment is overrun with lexicons, grammars, and how-tos for dozens of languages. In my free time, there's very little I'd rather do than sit down with a new primer, reveling in the dirty irregularities of language, the vestiges of history and culture and the fundamental human need to discuss scatological realities. I spend my weekends digging through Romanian, Mongolian, Cree. Occasionally, I watch Sylvester Stallone movies dubbed into Spanish. I really like flashcards.

I find language anything but boring. I love the patterns of language, the bits of grammatical code that take a series of sounds and make sense of them. I love new words, new sounds, new structure. But what I love best is this: each foreign language I study is both deeply familiar and entirely new. Every language has the same basic bits and pieces that I use every day. And every language puts those pieces together in a different—and oftentimes dazzling—way. For me, studying language is like having a never-ending supply of mind-blowing Pixies cover songs. I love the theme; I thrill to the variation.

I'm never going to be able to shove ninety-four languages fluently into my head. I'm always going to have trouble spitting out *il ristorante* or remembering to use the subjunctive when I need to use the subjunctive, even though the French subjunctive is different from the Greek subjunctive which is different from the English subjunctive. But with each new language I learn, I am—in a word—transported. To another culture, to another world. And for far less than the price of a plane ticket.

This is a best-of compilation, a collection of the quirks, innovations, and implausibilities of the world's languages—a jump-start for the novice word-traveler. I dug through languages I know and languages I'd never heard of, through dead languages and made-up languages and miserably difficult languages, all in search of the most interesting linguistic nooks and crannies. You won't find every language in here, just those that I happen to like best. Even so, there's plenty to talk about: language, like travel, is always stranger than you expect—and more beautiful than you ever imagined.

NOUNS

Like most people, I think about traveling far more than I actually do it. But even though I might not be able to afford a three-week trip to Japan, there is an upside to low income: the opportunity cost of a forty-minute daydream is pretty close to nil. So I don't feel too guilty about whiling away an afternoon making hypothetical plans for a trip I'll never take. I think about the cities I want to visit, the food I want to eat, the sites I want to see. I price transportation and look into visa requirements. And I write up language survival lists.

Because there's a difference between those of us who prefer books to people and those of us who actually manage to go out and do things—there's a reason, after all, that the CIA sorts out its analysts from its operatives. And I fall squarely on the analyst side, a bookworm with a deep-seated fear of social interaction. Put me in a crowd, and I can forget just about anything: science, trivia, history, my name. Not that the things I remember would be of much help, anyway. If I were ever to find myself in some life-threatening situation abroad, chances are I wouldn't be able to save myself by, say, being able to describe the proper uses of the future conditional. Which, in retrospect, might explain why the Agency never got back to me when I tried to apply. After all, what use would the CIA have for a budding linguist?

In any case, I make lists: Words I Should Know So I Don't Get Arrested; Words I Should Know So I Don't Get Mistaken for a Sex Worker; Words I Should Know So I Don't Die. And I keep the lists short. I stick with a few basic phrases I know I'll have reason to use—yes, I would like to see a doctor; no, I won't have your baby—and then I fill it out with the most necessary and useful part of speech: nouns. You

What's in a Noun

In third grade, I learned that a noun was "a person, place, or thing." Fair enough. But nouns aren't always so simple. If you're studying Mohawk, you might look up the word *ionta'araniiontahkhwa'* and find the nice, simple noun-like definition of "curtain." But, literally translated, *ionta'araniiontahkhwa'* is actually a combination of tiny word-pieces that mean "lace used to hang up." And in other languages, nouns can be smushed together to become entirely different parts of speech. In Chinese, the word *zhī* (知) means "knowledge." And *dào* (道) can mean "road" or "path." Put them together, though, and you get the verb *zhīdào* (知道): "to know." Sometimes you just can't rely on literal meaning to let you know what is a noun and what isn't—you have to look at context. When you're studying a new language, the "person, place, or thing" definition is about as helpful as describing food as "something that you eat."

know—water, beer, penicillin. That sort of thing. In my experience, a well-chosen noun and a bit of unambiguous body language can help get you through many a desperate moment.

But nouns are more than mere refuge for socially awkward obsessive-compulsives. In language, nouns are fascinating and complicated creatures, surprisingly fussy words that require all sorts of grammatical attention. Even so, when I first developed an interest in language, I didn't think much of nouns. In the brave new world of early language study, amidst exotic verbal constructions and uncharted phonemic territory, nouns seemed paltry, pedestrian. They were more the purview of strait-laced dictionaries, not the dense and mysterious grammars I had grown to love. For me, language study was nothing less than an adventure. And at first, the grammar of nouns seemed no more exciting than a trip to Delaware.

It wasn't the first time—nor will it be the last—that I was dead wrong.

NOUN CASE
My sophomore year of high school, I signed up for Ancient Greek. I did this in part because I was a big geek, but also because I needed an elective. And I can't paint to save my life.

The first week of class, my teacher turned to the chalkboard and wrote a bunch of different forms for the noun "country" like so:

Nom.	χώρα
Voc.	χώρα
Acc.	χώραν
Gen.	χώρας
Dat.	χώρᾳ

I was totally thrown. First of all, weren't we supposed to start with learning how to say our names? I'd been looking forward to choosing a pretty Greek name like Persephone or Calista.

What was worse, though, was that I had no clue as to why a language would need so many forms for some boring old noun. And all of the smug Latin students in my class did.

I had never regretted my lack of artistic ability more.

Thankfully, my teacher quickly explained that in Ancient Greek, noun endings indicate noun function—whether a noun is a subject, an object, or something else. So, the phrase "The country is great" would use the subject form χώρα (*chōra*), but "I betrayed my country" would use the object form χώραν (*chōran*).

It was then that I began to realize that nouns weren't quite the dullards I'd originally thought them to be. I was thrilled: in Ancient Greek, I wouldn't have to puzzle my way through word order and context to figure out the function of a noun. Instead, I could just look at the noun ending. To put it another way, if you have an Ancient Greek sentence that translates directly as, say, "Baby nobody in a corner puts," you'd know from the noun endings who was putting whom where even if you'd never seen *Dirty Dancing.*

This feature of Ancient Greek—and many other languages, including Latin, German, Russian, and even English, back in the day—is known as "noun declension." It's a lot like verb conjugation, except instead of changing the verb to agree with its subject, you're changing the noun to agree with its function, or *case.* But never, ever call it "noun conjugation"— unless you're trying to needle a bratty language snob. Verbs conjugate, nouns decline.

But I don't want to bore you with too much terminology. Quickly, then, like ripping off a Band-Aid, the most common noun cases: the nominative form of the noun is used to mark the subject. The vocative is used when you're addressing the noun in question. In English, we usually place a comma after a noun that's used as a vocative ("Girl, you know it's true"). The accusative is used for the direct object of the verb, while the dative is used for, among other things, the indirect object. And the genitive marks possession or a close relationship—to translate a noun in the genitive case into English, it's often easiest to plunk down an "of" before it, as in the Statue of Liberty—or the International House of Pancakes.

So if you're in Red Square and you're in the mood for some history, you wouldn't head for the mausoleum of the nominative Ленин (*Lenin*), but

---

Babes in Iceland

Common nouns aren't the only nouns subject to considerations of case. Proper names, too, get the grammatical treatment. Which is all well and good until parents decide that they want their kids to be *special*. And then all of a sudden, schoolteachers around the country have to struggle to figure out the genitive of Suri, Shiloh, *Kal-El*. Iceland, for one, is having none of it. If you want to use a nontraditional baby name in Iceland, you must first pass it by the Icelandic Naming Committee. New names can't contain any non-Icelandic letters, and they have to be amenable to Icelandic declension patterns. And if the Committee turns down your request, you're shit out of luck. If you're a celebrity interested in emigrating to Iceland, consider yourself forewarned.

rather the genitive Ленина (*Lenina*). If you spot a rug while shopping in Turkey, you don't ask to buy the nominative *halı*, you ask to buy the accusative *halıyı*. And in Iceland, if your family were laying a guilt trip on you about staying in touch, you wouldn't send an e-mail to your nominative *móðir*, but to your dative *móður*.

Noun case is even wilder the wider you cast your linguistic net. Serbo-Croatian has a locative case that indicates—as you might expect—location. Russian has an instrumental case that marks the object with which an action is carried out, as in "I hit him with a rock," or "killing me softly with his song." Tlingit, a nearly extinct language spoken in parts of Alaska and western Canada, has cases that I don't even understand: punctual, pertingent, prolative. I suspect that a full analysis of Tlingit nouns would require a space-time sophistication far beyond anyone with my mediocre math and science skills.

A language family with a famously rigorous case system is the Uralic family, a group of languages that includes Estonian, Finnish, and Hungarian. I was aware of the perils of Finnish before I even knew about case, having once asked a friend what he thought the hardest language in the world must be. He pointed to Finnish. "They don't really have prepositions," he told me, abject terror in his eyes. "Just different sets of noun endings. *Dozens* of them."

I can only imagine my reaction on the first day of class had I chosen a Finnish—or, worse, Hungarian—elective back in high school. In Hungarian, many nouns are declined for a full *eighteen* cases: nominative, accusative, dative-genitive, instrumental, causal-final, translative, terminative, essive-formal, essive-modal, inessive, superessive, adessive, illative, allative, sublative, elative, delative, and ablative. If English were to decline the word "bar" using the Hungarian system, it might look something roughly like this:

barás	the bar (subject)
bart	the bar (object)
barásnak	to the bar
barással	with the bar
barásért	for the bar
barássá	into the bar
barásig	as far as the bar
barásként	as the bar
barásul	by way of the bar

barásban	in the bar
baráson	on the bar
barásnál	at the bar
barásba	into the bar
barásra	onto the bar
baráshoz	to the bar
barásból	out of the bar
barásról	about the bar
barástól	from the bar

Now, imagine coming home from the aforementioned watering hole and having to explain to your significant other exactly where you were and what you were doing all night—in Hungarian. Frankly, if my romantic life were dependent on an ability to successfully navigate eighteen noun cases, I'd have to do a 180 on my longtime dating strategy and give up alcohol entirely.

Despite my friend's grim warnings, however, Uralic nouns aren't, relatively speaking, so bad. The endings are blessedly regular, and there are only one or two possible endings per case. So once you get past the initial shock, learning to decline a Hungarian or Finnish noun isn't terribly different from memorizing a list of prepositions. Lithuanian, on the other hand (which has a paltry six cases by comparison), has different sets of endings for different kinds of nouns. A noun that ends in -is in the nominative will have a genitive ending of -io—but a noun that ends in -a in the nominative takes the genitive ending -os. And so on, and so on, and so on—and I haven't even gotten to the separate plural endings. Even if you just want to be able to decline *regular* nouns in Lithuanian, you have to learn more than 150 endings.

Native English-speakers spend a lot of time thanking their lucky stars that they grew up speaking English—and, yes, it's great in that it's a widely spoken language, and I'm certainly personally grateful that I didn't have to go through school to enjoy *Rocky* in its original, glorious language. (Although I have at times wondered if the film's dialogue might not qualify as a separate dialect.) But whenever I see Lithuanian nouns, I can't help but think: I kind of wish I'd grown up speaking Lithuanian. Everything else would seem so simple after that.

If I had to choose a language with a genuinely terrifying level of noun complexity, I'd skip right over Finland, Hungary, and Lithuania and head to the border between France and Spain, in the crook of the Bay of Biscay. There, nearly a million people

....

Despite its lonely genetic classification, the Basque language has been anything but isolated over the years. Although the Basque people certainly never took to the sea as the Spanish and Portuguese did, they were nonetheless extremely accomplished fishermen and seafarers, and by the sixteenth century they were sailing regularly to the New World. In fact, some scholars actually believe that Basque traders managed to make it to North America before Columbus did. Regardless, it's clear that they spent plenty of time in and around the St. Lawrence River: when Jacques Cartier rolled up in 1542, he found that many of the locals could actually speak a simplified form of Basque.

speak Basque, or *Euskara*, a language beloved by enthusiasts for its unusual sound and structure.

Most European languages share a single, distant ancestor—the ancient and now reconstructed language known as Indo-European. This means that even though English and Lithuanian aren't at all mutually intelligible, they do share certain basic linguistic features. Basque, however, is what's known as a language isolate. Although experts have been able to dig up Basque's immediate ancestor, the ancient language known as Aquitanian, as of yet, no one's been able to identify a genetic link with any other modern language. So in the universe of human speech, Basque's pretty much in a world all its own.

As a result, Basque has a number of grammatical features that seem downright kooky to anyone who didn't grow up with the language. Even something as basic as word order can be compellingly different. Basque verbs, for instance, often show up at the end of a sentence: *Amerikanoa naiz*—"I'm American." With a negative statement, though, the verb gets shunted to the front: *Ez naiz amerikanoa.*

Basque nouns are particularly complex. Basque has eleven grammatical cases, most of which correspond to English prepositions—the benefactive case, for example, can be translated with an English "for," as in "I did it all for you." Each case suffix has a number of forms depending on whether it's tacked onto a consonant or a vowel and whether the noun is singu-

BITING THE WAX TADPOLE

lar or plural, definite or indefinite. But the case endings aren't, as you might expect, necessarily tacked onto the noun in question—in Basque you put a case marker after the entire noun phrase. If you want to say "in the house," then, you would use the inessive form of house: *etxean*. But if you wanted to say "in the *pretty* house," you would put the case marker on the adjective: *etxe politean*—literally, "house pretty-in-the."

Despite its genetic isolation, however, one of Basque's most intriguing grammatical quirks is shared by a number of other languages throughout the world, including Tagalog, Tibetan, and Sumerian. These languages distinguish between two kinds of subject nouns: subjects of transitive verbs (verbs that take an object) and subjects of intransitive verbs (verbs that do not). In Basque, each type of subject noun takes a different noun case. In the nineteenth century, this feature was referred to as a "double nominative," a rare bit of confusing grammatical terminology that didn't manage to lodge itself permanently in modern grammar texts. Today, these two cases are known, respectively, as ergative and absolutive.

What's particularly challenging about ergative and absolutive constructions is that direct objects are also marked with the absolutive case. In the sentences *ardoa beltza da* and *ardoa nahi du*, the word for wine (*ardoa*) looks exactly the same. And yet in the first sentence, *ardoa* is the subject: "The wine is red." In the second, it's the object: "He wants wine." When speaking Basque, then, you have to do away with the fundamental subject-object distinction that you learned in elementary school: in Basque, objects look like subjects.

Mastering the use of the ergative and absolutive in Basque isn't just a matter of memorizing noun endings and transitive and intransitive verbs. It's also a matter of coming to grips with a structure that just feels unnatural to speakers of most languages. At the end of the day, trying to learn Basque is pretty much the linguistic equivalent of transferring to a high school where the cheerleaders date the chess club.

NOUN CONTEXT

Of course, noun case isn't the only tool in the linguistic box with regard to noun function. If it were, English would be roundly screwed. In many languages, English included, the function of a noun depends in large part on word order. Consider the phrase *Joanie loves Chachi*. English-speakers need no extra information to figure who's loving whom; if you grew up with the language, then you've been hard-wired to look at a sentence and translate the word order as subject, verb, object.

The most common word order among the world's languages, however, is Subject-Object-Verb. In an

SOV language—Persian or Hindi, perhaps—Joanie doesn't love Chachi, instead *Joanie Chachi loves*. There are plenty of examples of Verb-Subject-Object, too: Welsh, Ancient Egyptian, and Maori are all *loves Joanie Chachi* languages. (For some reason, it's this particular alignment that stretches my own linguistic flexibility to breaking. Every time I try to learn Scottish Gaelic, an otherwise not inordinately difficult language, I fail miserably. I can't help but think that it has something to do with my distinctly Scottish predisposition for self-sabotage.)

Although the vast majority of the world's languages rely more or less on one of these three templates, there are, here and there, even more differently ordered languages. Chances are you won't run

Happy Days

As legend has it, when *Joanie Loves Chachi* aired in Korea, it was Korea's highest-rated American television show ever—due not, as you'd might expect, to the considerable charms of Scott Baio, but rather to a delightful bit of homophony. Although the ratings claim appears to have been a bit of an exaggeration, you don't need to be a television executive to see why the title in translation might be a substantial improvement on the original: in Korean, "Chachi" sounds an awful lot like a slang word for "penis."

into them unless you're traveling to remote areas of Brazil—or, possibly, to a sci-fi convention. Klingon, which was designed by the linguist Marc Okrand to be as alien as possible, uses the reverse of the English order: *Chachi loves Joanie.*

Although word order is relatively fixed in English, some languages can pretty much play fast and loose with it. Latin and Greek use inflection to dump all sorts of useful grammatical information into each noun, so if a poet wants to right the rhythm of a line or an orator needs to emphasize an object, they can switch up a few nouns without sacrificing meaning. You don't have to be a romantic, then, to know the true meaning of *omnia vincit amor*—literally, "all conquers love."

Another way languages put nouns in their place is through the use of helpful little words like prepositions—which, perhaps surprisingly, have their own restrictions regarding word order. One French phrase that, as far as I can tell, every beginning student is forced to learn, is *le livre est sur la table*—"The book is on the table." Had I ever believed my textbook to have the slightest interest in real-world applications, I would surely have been convinced that France was a country entirely without bookshelves. The prepositional phrase here is just like it is in English: the preposition *sur* comes before *la table*, the noun it refers to. The same sentence in Tibetan, however, is *chogtse ki ghang la teb du*: literally, "the table on book is."

In Tibetan and many other languages with a Subject-Object-Verb order, prepositions come *after* nouns—which is why they're properly called "postpositions."

Many languages also sort out their nouns with words known as "particles." The term "particle" encompasses a wide variety of tiny, invariable words that perform some kind of grammatical function. The lines between particles, prepositions, and even articles, however, aren't always clear and tend to vary from language to language and linguist to linguist. Particles in English are particularly tough to pin down. A few relatively clear-cut examples are the preposition-like words used in verb compounds: shut up, cheer up, put up. Which, admittedly, isn't very exciting in a grammatical sense—unless you're a copyeditor or channeling Winston Churchill. In other languages, however, particles are kind of magic, pointing out subjects or objects or comments or questions with very little hassle.

Particles often offer a glimpse into the conversational subtleties of a language. In Japanese, two separate particles can be used to identify the lead noun of a sentence. The particle は (*wa*) marks the topic of a sentence, and the particle が (*ga*) marks the subject of sentence. Both particles are like grammatically pointed mean-girl fingers: see that word over there? I'm going to talk about it right now. But *wa* emphasizes the topic's comment, whereas *ga* emphasizes the subject. So you'd use *wa* if the gossip is the juiciest bit ("She *had an alien baby*"), but you'd use *ga* if the subject is ("*Angelina Jolie* had an alien baby").

In Maori, the particles *a* and *o* can link two nouns in a possessive relationship, much like the English preposition "of." But English doesn't distinguish between types of possession—"of" can be used with cars, books, clothes, husbands. In some languages, however—such as Lao, spoken in Laos—alienable (my shoes) and inalienable (my soul) possession require separate grammatical constructions. And Maori has an even more complicated point of view: permanence isn't the issue at hand; control is. The particle *a* is used to describe a relationship you're in control of, like perhaps your relationship with your household pets. Meanwhile, the particle *o* is used for a relationship you're not in control of, like maybe your relationship with your parents—provided, that is, that your family's anything like mine.

NOUN NUMBER

At one time, the mere notion of noun number was enough to send me into a near-catatonic state of ennui—if I didn't care for nouns, then you can imagine how I felt about multiples of nouns. The truth of the matter, though, is that throughout the world, language is so restlessly diverse that even noun number turns out to exhibit unexpected grammatical delights.

The first, and simplest, aspect of grammatical number is the way a language distinguishes between a singular and a plural. To indicate plural number in English, typically all you have to do is add an -s to the end of a word. Turns out, a few other big-time languages often do the same—French, Spanish, Portuguese—which is rather convenient.

But it's not always so easy. Even in English, a language of limited inflection, there are tons of irregular plurals. There are, for instance, words that end in "f" that take a "v" in the plural like calves, halves, elves. (And yet: "roofs.") English also has tricky plurals like children and oxen, geese, teeth, and feet. And then there's the Latinate plural—alumnus and alumni, addendum and addenda—which has gained enough highbrow language-maven currency over the centuries that I find myself regularly questioning the plural of walrus.

So it should come as no surprise that throughout the world, languages have a number of ways—some simple, some elaborate—to mark plural nouns. On the simpler side are those languages that use particles for plurals, like Tagalog, which uses the particle *mga* to indicate the plural of common nouns: *mga batà*, "the children." Malay and Indonesian, two very closely related languages, often form plurals with reduplication. To form the plural of a word, just repeat it: in Malay, *anak*, "child," becomes *anak-anak*, "children"; and *buku*, "book," becomes *buku-buku*, "books."

A Collective of Nouns

A plural noun is different from a collective noun—a noun that refers to a group of items, as in "deck of cards" or "pack of wild dogs." Many languages also have special ways to mark collective nouns grammatically.

Javanese uses reduplication, or repetition of the word, for its collective nouns, while Navajo can insert a verb prefix to indicate that an action is being performed by a group. Some of the most unusual collective nouns, however, are actually found in English, which has somehow developed a truly bizarre collection of species-specific collective nouns: a murder of crows, a mess of iguanas, and—my favorite—a coffle of asses.

A language family with a notably tricky plural is the Semitic family, which includes the modern languages Arabic and Hebrew, not to mention Aramaic, Ancient Egyptian, Akkadian, and Phoenician. Semitic languages are—and I don't think I'm exaggerating here—awesome. Whereas many languages rely on word endings to get the grammatical gist across, Semitic languages instead let the internal vowels do the heavy lifting. (This grammatical curiosity notwithstanding, Semitic scripts often omit vowels, which I find wonderfully perverse.)

Semitic grammar is based in large part on word roots of three consonants. Each root has a general meaning, and by adding and changing the vowels between the consonants, you can create related nouns, verbs, and adjectives. And once you learn one derivational pattern, you can use it over and over again. Take the Arabic root *ktb*, which is associated with writing. By using different vowel patterns, by lengthening or changing the vowels, you can derive other writing-related words like *kataba*, "he wrote," *kātib*, "writer," or *kitāb*, "book."

And if you see another related word—*maktaba*, for instance, which means "library"—you can work backwards to find the pattern and then apply it to another root. In the case of *maktaba*, you can deduce that by adding the prefix *ma-* to a root and tacking on an *a* to each of the last two consonants, you can derive the word for a place where the root activity happens. Which means that then you can take another root—say, *drs*, "to study"—and make a new word with the same pattern: *madrasa*, "school."

The patterns of vowel change do tend to make plurals a bit of a pain, though. In Semitic languages, there are two ways to form a plural. The first is known as the "sound plural," which consists of adding an ending to a word, Indo-European-style. In Arabic, one set of endings (*-ūn* or *-īn*, depending on the noun case) is used primarily with nouns that refer to men or groups of men: *mudarris*, "male teacher," *mudarrisūn*, "male teachers." Another ending (*-āt*) is used for groups of women and for a variety of other nouns, regardless of gender: *mudarrisa*, "female teacher," *mudarrisāt*, "female teachers." Notice that each of these words has the consonants *drs* contained within them, so even if you didn't know what the words meant, you could guess that they had something to do with study. Which, again: awesome.

Some words, however, have plural forms based on internal vowel change, forms known as "broken plurals"—presumably because you have to break up the singular and stick the consonants together with new vowels to form a plural.

To form a broken plural, you have to pick out the root consonants of a singular form and then fit the consonants into the proper plural pattern:

SINGULAR	ROOT	PATTERN	PLURAL
kitāb (book)	*ktb*	1-u-2-u-3	*kutub* (books)
bayt (house)	*byt*	1-u-2-ū-3	*buyūt* (houses)
kalb (dog)	*klb*	1-i-2-ā-3	*kilāb* (dogs)

These forms aren't so different in theory from ir-regular English plurals like goose and geese, but in Arabic in particular, broken plural forms tend to be the rule, not the exception—even if the rules governing the changes aren't exactly easy to master. My Arabic grammars assure me that eventually I will get a "feel" for which nouns take which broken plural patterns, a maddeningly common circumlocution in language texts for "this shit is hard." For the most part, though, learning Arabic plurals entails some seriously laborious rote memorization. Which, admittedly, somewhat undermines my fondness for Semitic inflection.

In other parts of the world, grammatical number is more than a plain-Jane distinction between "one" and "more than one." Many languages also have dual forms used for groups of exactly two: some languages use it for any group of two; other languages use it for items that come naturally in pairs, like shoes or underwhelming political candidates. In Hopi, *taaqa* means "one man," *taaqavit* means "two men," and *taataqt* means "three or more men." Slovenian also has a dual number: *mesto*, "city"; *mesti*, "two cities"; *mesta*, "three or more cities." (In Slovenian, however, anything that occurs in a natural pair is put in the plural.)

A language that is inordinately fond of the dual is Sanskrit. Any noun in Sanskrit, regardless of whether it comes naturally in a pair, can be expressed in the dual number.

aśvaḥ "horse"	*aśvau* "two horses"	*aśvāḥ* "three or more horses"
nadī "river"	*nadyau* "two rivers"	*nadyaḥ* "three or more rivers"
godhuk "cowmilker"	*goduhau* "two cowmilkers"	*godhugbhiḥ* "three or more cowmilkers"

The dual is also used with the ubiquitous Sanksrit noun compound *dvandva*, which means, literally, "couple." In a *dvandva* compound, nouns are joined so as to do away with silly things like a word for "and," as in *ācāryaśiṣyau* "teacher and student." Despite the linguistic nomenclature, however, *dvandva* compounds are by no means limited to groups of two. You can, for example, take the singular nouns *aśvaḥ* (horse), *gajaḥ* (elephant), *bālaḥ* (child), and *narāḥ* (man) and smash them together to form *aśvagajabālanarāḥ*: "horses, elephants, children, and men." And there's no limit to how many nouns you can string together. Just as German has a tendency to string nouns together to form words of intimidating length, so Sanskrit has little fear of noun compounds that just keep on going.

In some languages, grammatical number is even more particular. Larike, a language spoken on Ambon Island in eastern Indonesia, has a trial number, used for groups of three. In Baiso, a language spoken by about a thousand people in southwestern Ethiopia, nouns can take a form called a "paucal"—a word that doesn't even show up in *Merriam-Webster*, so you can probably imagine how widespread this construction is. The paucal bridges the gap between singular and plural—it's kind of like a grammatical indicator for "a few." But unlike the dual and the trial, the exact definition of paucal number varies from language to language. In Baiso, the paucal is used for small numbers of individuals, usually between two and six. In Fijian, however, the paucal can be used for numbers up to thirty.

Grammatical number may not seem to be the sexiest side of language, but anything that equates twenty-nine with "a few" seems awfully liberated indeed.

Seriously, German Nouns are Ridiculous

Rechtsschutzversicherungsgesellschaften, "insurance companies that provide legal protection"

Rindfleischetikettierungsüberwachungsaufgabenübertragungsgesetz, "beef labeling regulation and delegation of supervision law"

Donaudampfschiffahrtskapitänswitwe, "widow of the captain of the Danube steamship line"

CLASS

In many of the world's languages, different kinds of nouns take different kinds of adjectives, articles, and pronouns. If words are pieces of clothing, then these languages assign different colors to different words. And grammar—the Anna Wintour in this metaphor, if you will—dictates that your clothes have to match. If you have a violet noun, you have to make sure you use a violet adjective. Of course, you *could* combine a forest-green noun with a chartreuse adjective, but it would be ugly and people would probably laugh at you.

When languages divvy up their words in this way and ask you to accessorize your nouns with eye- and grammar-pleasing modifiers, they have what is known as noun "class." English-speakers know noun class better by another name: the dread and politically contentious grammatical "gender."

The first day of any beginning Spanish or French class is more often than not marked by a number of incredulous looks as students wonder just why a chair is a girl and a book is a boy. Cultural anthropology aside, there's nothing inherently feminine or masculine about many of the words that are classed as feminine or masculine, and, in fact, if you assume a consistent correlation between natural gender and grammatical gender, you're in for a bit of a shock.

Grammatical gender often appears to be based on just the right combination of reason and utterly arbitrary dart-throwing monkey logic to ensure maximum confusion. In French, a woman's blouse is the masculine *chemisier* while a man's dress shirt is the feminine *chemise*. In German, famously, the word for girl—*Madchën*—is neuter. And in Old English, *wīfman*, the word for woman, was masculine.

Grammatical gender and natural gender don't always match up for one simple reason: grammatical gender was made up. Sometime in the fifth century B.C., a Greek philosopher named Protagoras was trying to puzzle out the way that language worked. He saw that Greek nouns came in, more or less, three different groups, and so, for lack of a better idea, he called the groups "masculine," "feminine," and "neuter."

He quickly realized that his taxonomy might be a bit misleading: according to Aristotle, Protagoras was concerned that manly words like "helmet" and "anger" actually fell onto the feminine side of things. So whenever you're looking at a foreign-language dictionary, wondering why the word for "underwire" is masculine, just know that the guy who came up with the system would have been right there with you.

The word "gender," by the way, comes from the Latin *genus,* which means "kind" or "sort" and originally had nothing at all to do with reproductive anatomy or the historical oppression of anyone with the bad luck to be stuck with a set of ovaries.

Even so, noun class is a veritable cornucopia of tempting term-paper material for the armchair anthropologist. In Amharic, an Ethiopian language closely related to Arabic and Hebrew, gender is aligned with size and sensitivity: a feminine article tacked onto a masculine noun can indicate diminutive size or tender feeling. As a masculine form, *betu* means "the house." As a feminine form, *betitu* means "the little house." Nama, a Khoisan language spoken primarily in Namibia, has a trans-gender: nouns of one gender will sometimes take on the ending of another gender to indicate unusual size. And perhaps the most celebrated and suggestive class system is found in Dyirbal, a nearly extinct Australian aboriginal language. Dyirbal was made famous when linguist George Lakoff titled one of his books after three components of a single Dyirbal noun class: *Women, Fire, and Dangerous Things.*

But before you go publishing a paper on the gender politics of language, remember the plight of Protagoras: sometimes the real sociological troublemaker isn't language itself, but rather the way we choose to describe language.

Noun class extends well beyond a feminine/masculine distinction. Linguists speculate that Proto-Indo-European originally distinguished between animate and inanimate, and only later did the animate class separate out into masculine and feminine nouns. Many other languages, including Bengali and

Hittite, distinguish between living creatures and inanimate objects. Ojibwe, an Algonquin language, also separates animate from inanimate nouns, but in Ojibwe, "animate" doesn't always mean what you might expect it to. A stone, for instance, is classed as animate. So too are tobacco, money, and bread.

Funny little rules about animacy also come into play in the Slavic languages. In Russian, two nouns that otherwise might share the same declension pattern can have different forms in the accusative, depending on whether or not the nouns are living. So even though their endings *should* look the same, the accusative of "king" is короля (*korolja*), and the accusative of "car" is автомобиль (*avtomobil'*). This only occurs, however, with masculine nouns: grammatically, the language couldn't care less if the ladies are living or dying. Which may or may not inspire some good-natured speculation about the sociological implications of privileged male animacy.

Other languages divide their nouns into rational and irrational classes. In Sumerian, for instance, people and gods comprised one class, and everything else comprised the irrational class. Tamil, a language spoken in India, Malaysia, Sri Lanka, and Singapore, classifies its nouns in the same way. Curiously, though, the distinction in Old Tamil was between animate and inanimate nouns—which means that at some point, animals got demoted. I'm sure the change resulted from a phonological shift, but I like

RIISMO

THE LANGUAGE FORMERLY KNOWN AS ESPERANTO

The Pronoun Game

Esperanto, the language launched in 1887 by L. L. Zamenhof, has provoked a great deal of criticism on account of what some consider to be a deeply sexist structure—an unacceptable situation, it is argued, on account of the fact that Esperanto is a wholly made-up language. One of the main bones of contention regards the adoption of the gender-neutral pronoun *ri*. Reformers consider this so necessary to their cause that they have named their gender-neutral version of Esperanto *"Riismo."* Whether the Riists manage to have a lasting impact on Esperanto remains to be seen, but they certainly seem to be having better luck than anyone's ever had with English.

to think that somewhere in the history of Tamil was a singularly bad dog.

Noun class is particularly important in the Bantu language family, an extremely diverse group of languages that includes Swahili, Zulu, and Xhosa. Noun class affects nearly every aspect of a Bantu sentence: nouns, verbs, and pronouns are all pulled into alignment by the force of not one, not two, but as many as *twenty-two* noun classes. If you've ever bitched about gender in French or Spanish, you might want to reconsider your feelings on the matter right about now.

But even though double-digit noun classes are the stuff of student nightmares, Bantu noun class works like a dream. Consider Swahili: each noun is marked with one of sixteen appropriate prefixes, and any verbs, adjectives, and pronouns associated with it take a coordinating (and occasionally alliterative) prefix—which means that at times, even with everyday words, Swahili just sings:

watu	*watu wazuri*	*watu wazuri wawili*
people	good people	two good people
viatu	*viatu vizuri*	*viatu vizuri viwili*
shoes	good shoes	two good shoes

Swahili noun class is also incredibly productive. By switching out one prefix for another, you can change a noun's number or meaning in a predictable—and satisfying—way. One noun class, for instance, contains all singular plants; another contains plural plants. So by changing the *mn-* prefix of *mnanasi* (pineapple plant) to *min*, you can form a plural: *minanasi* (pineapple plants). And because fruit is associated with another class, you can just switch out the prefix again to create a slightly different meaning: *nanasi* (pineapple); *mananasi* (pineapples).

Every time I study Swahili, I can't help thinking about systems of measurement. Despite my Canadian half-parentage, I'm not so good with the metric system—I'm clueless when it comes to grams or liters or degrees Celsius. A Buddhist monk in China once asked me my height in meters, and I told him three. (Yes: I told him I was ten feet tall.) But even though I have no feel for metric units, I can still look at its conversion charts and marvel at its elegance. It has sense, it has logic. It does not have 5,280 feet to the mile.

Swahili is the metric system of languages. Like any language, it has its irregularities, but once you figure out a few prefix patterns, you can derive all sorts of words. For example, many country names start with the letter "u." But if you switch out the "u" for an "m" or "w," the word can then refer to the citizen or citizens of that country. Or, if you want to talk about language, you can switch out the "u" for the prefix *ki-*, which means "in the manner of."

Ufaransa	*Mfaransa*	*Wafaransa*	*Kifaransa*
France	French man	French men	French
Uchina	*Mchina*	*Wachina*	*Kichina*
China	Chinese man	Chinese men	Chinese
Urusi	*Mrusi*	*Warusi*	*Kirusi*
Russia	Russian man	Russian men	Russian

The sheer size of the Bantu class system means that it can't possibly be easy to figure out. In language, as in life, complexity can be overwhelming at first. But under closer inspection, it can prove to be something sublime.

VERBS

When I was eleven or twelve years old, I somehow got my hands on a copy of an audio course in German. The course was designed to get diplomats up to speed as soon as possible: it didn't bother so much with individual words as it did complete sentences. So after only a few days, I was carefully repeating phrases designed to get me between the airport and the embassy as quickly as possible. The first sentence I managed to commit to memory—and that today is basically all I remember of my spoken German— was somewhat less practical. The sentence was *Ich möchte gern Zigaretten haben*: I'd like to have some cigarettes. As this was followed soon thereafter by *Das Bier ist sehr gut*, it's no wonder that I wanted to be a diplomat for most of high school: my German course made foreign service sound like a frat party.

I must have repeated the first phrase to my father at some point, because he took the time to point out to me how the verb *haben* was shunted to the end: a more literal translation is "I would like some cigarettes to have." He explained that this often happens in German, and to illustrate this he told me the following joke: An American woman goes to Berlin to hear Otto von Bismarck speak in the Reichstag. But, being American, the woman doesn't speak German, so she hires a translator to come to the speech with her. Bismarck begins, and the woman breathlessly awaits the translation. Much to her dismay, however, her translator remains silent. The speech continues, and the woman grows ever more agitated: the translator still has yet to say a single word. Eventually, she loses her patience, gives the translator a discreet shove, and asks him just what, exactly, he thinks he's doing. The translator turns to her and replies, "Madam, I am waiting for the verb."

Verbs are traditionally defined as words that express an action, an occurrence, or existence. I prefer the far more evocative Dutch translation: *werkwoord*—"work-word." Because verbs aren't just the words that communicate what work is being done in a sentence, they're also the words that handle the bulk of the grammatical workload. And so, verbs are the ringleaders of a sentence, irrepressible gossips that dish all the best dirt: who's acting, who's being acted on; when the action takes place, how long the action lasts; and, most astoundingly, how the speaker feels about that action.

However, just like real-life gossips, verbs can also be a bit of a pain in the ass. It can take a great deal of time and concerted effort to slog through the linguistic morass of verbal construction. If you search long enough, though, you may be surprised by what you find. In language, as in Berlin, verbs are worth the wait.

CONJUGATION AND COPULATION

Not too long ago, I found myself talking to a high school student about his upcoming class schedule. Because I can really only talk about three things (language, pop culture, my inability to make small talk), I asked him if he was planning on taking a language class his senior year. He told me he wasn't—

he'd stopped taking Spanish as soon as he'd fulfilled his class requirement. "But why?" I asked. "What's so bad about Spanish?"

He gave me the same look I used to give my mom when she asked me what was so wrong with wearing a sweater set and said, "Conjugation."

Nobody likes conjugating verbs. Except for me, maybe, but I'm well aware that I'm an anomaly. Even so, if you look past the pain and suffering of memorization and recitation, conjugation can point the way toward a number of interesting facts about the way that verbs work—and the languages they work in.

Anyone who has studied a Romance language knows that different languages require different kinds of verb conjugations. English verbs have only two forms: one for the third-person singular ("She dances") and one for everything else ("I/you/we/they dance"). Spanish, though, has six distinct verb forms, one each in the singular and plural for the first, second, and third person: *bailo, bailas, baila, bailamos, bailáis, bailan.* In Bengali, one of the most widely spoken Indo-European languages, number doesn't affect verb conjugation—I and we, you and y'all, and he and they each take the same verb forms. Speakers of Bengali do, however, have to take into account their relationships to whomever they're addressing, as there are three forms of increasing respect: one for close friends, one for general acquaintances, and one for polite situations.

Basque, Inuktitut, and Mapudungun, the language of the Mapuche in Chile and Argentina, are known as polypersonal languages. In these languages, verb conjugations take into account not only the subjects of the verb, but also the objects. Which means that a phrase like "I gave it to him" can be contained in a single word—*elufiñ* in Mapudungun, for instance.

The Tangut language is a particularly unusual case. In the tenth century, the Tangut people established a state in the area that now comprises the western Chinese provinces of Shaanxi, Gansu, and Ningxia. For the next two hundred years or so, the dynasty, commonly known by its Chinese name *Xixia* (or Western Xia), flourished. And then Genghis Khan showed up.

Suffice it to say, today Tangut only exists in museum collections and library archives.

Tangut verbs are unusual because they can agree with either the subject *or* the object, depending on the context. In a sentence like "I shot a man in Reno just to watch him die," the verb "shot" would agree with the subject—just as in English. But in the equally likely Tangut sentence "My baby shot me down," the verb would agree with "me," the object. In both cases, even though the subjects are very different, the verb form would actually remain the same.

Then there are copulas, verbs that link nouns with adjectives, predicates, or other nouns. Which is to say, primarily verbs that translate as "to be." In

English, we use the verb "to be" to express all kinds of states, circumstantial and essential, temporary and permanent: I am cold; I am cold-hearted; I am drunk; I am a drunk. But in some languages, you have to be more precise. Guaraní, one of the official languages of Paraguay, has two verbs that translate as "I am." The first verb, *aime*, is used solely to describe location, as in "I am at the concert." The second verb, *aiko*, can be used as "to be" only in certain idiomatical constructions. If someone asks how you are doing in Guaraní, you would reply *"Aiko porã"*—I'm fine. But if you want to describe something as old or mean or blue, you wouldn't use a verb at all. Instead, you can just put the adjective right next to the subject: *xe*

Al Gore
mburuvicharangue

Noun Tense

A particularly unusual feature of Guaraní is its use of tense—but not with relation to verbs, with relation to nouns. Guaraní nouns can be marked with two different endings, -kue or -ra. *Kue* is a past-tense marker, similar to the English prefix ex-, and *ra* is a future-tense marker. So if you consider the word for "president," *mburuvicha*, then Bill Clinton is a *mburuvichakue*, and Barack Obama is a potential *mburuvichara*. You can also combine the endings: *mburuvicharangue* means "what we thought was going to be a future president but then turned out not to be." In other words: Al Gore.

BITING THE WAX TADPOLE

tujama, xe vai, xe hovy. "I am old, I am mean, I am blue." (Apparently, my sources on Guaraní are less well suited for me than they are for a particularly unpleasant incarnation of Papa Smurf.)

Guaraní isn't the only language with more than one way to say "to be." In Italian, "I am American" is "*Sono americana.*" (Or *americano*, if you're a guy.) But if someone asks how you're doing (*Come stai?*), you'd use a different verb to say "I'm fine": *Sto bene.* These two Italian verbs, *essere* and *stare*, have the same English translation—"to be"—but they're subtly different in meaning. *Essere* is used to describe identity, essence—any fundamental characteristic. *Stare*, on the other hand, is used to describe feelings, appearance.

In English, this distinction can often be captured by replacing "to be" with "to look" or "to feel."

Essere:	*Sei bella.*	"You are beautiful."
Stare:	*Stai bella.*	"You look beautiful."

This distinction can be traced back, unsurprisingly, to Latin. Italian, as you might expect, is often very close to Latin in terms of vocabulary, and any Latin student would immediately recognize that these two Italian verbs are derived from the Latin verbs *esse* and *stāre*. Now, *esse* is the Latin verb "to be," so that makes perfect sense. *Stāre*, on the other hand, primarily means "to stand." However, over time, words eventually start meaning more than just their dictionary definitions, particularly in a culture that likes poetry as much as the Romans did. So eventually *stare* began to be used from time to time as something closer to the English "stand," as in "I stand corrected." By the time colloquial Latin (affectionately known as "vulgar," which originally meant "in ordinary use") spread throughout Europe, both verbs could mean "to be."

As a result, most Romance languages have multiple forms of "to be," each with its own subtle meaning—Spanish, Portuguese, and Catalan all distinguish between *ser*, "to be," and *estar*, "to look or feel." French, thanks to its tendency to undergo pronunciation shifts that make its words all sound the same, has merged the two forms, so that today there is only one verb—*être*—for both states of being.

Several Celtic languages also feature multiple copulas. For example, the two words in Scottish Gaelic that can translate as "to be" are *tha* and *is*. One Gaelic grammar I have—the optimistically named *Gaelic Without Groans*—tells me to think of *is* as the equivalent of 'tis. I have no idea what that's supposed to mean.

Old English also had a few words for "to be," but, unlike Spanish and Italian (and Scottish Gaelic—I think), the meaning of each copula was relatively interchangeable, so eventually the different forms got rolled together. If you've ever wondered why the English conjugation of "to be" is so seemingly random, this is why. From *bēon*, the "official" infinitive form, we get the modern forms "to be," "been," and the imperative "be." Another verb, *wesan*, gave us the forms "was" and "were." And a third verb, which shares the same Indo-European root as the Latin *esser*, is responsible for "am" and "is."

TENSE AND ASPECT

One of my favorite language quotes of all time comes from William Safire, who once noted that "only in language can you be more than perfect." What a lovely remark—it's the sort of thing I'd half expect to see at the top of Mr. Safire's MySpace page, if he had one. (Likes: Words, words, words, Abe Lincoln. Dislikes: Nattering, nabobs, negativism.)

The quip refers to the English pluperfect—from the Latin *plūs quam perfectum*, literally, "more than perfect"—the tense we use when we want to describe an action that was completed *before* another past action: I had already done it by the time he told me not to. As it turns out, though, tense is actually anything but perfect—at least with regard to language study. Along with verbal aspect (which I'll get to) verb tense is one of the most challenging grammatical concepts to get a handle on.

Tense derives from the Latin *tempus*, "time" (as opposed to the Latin *tensus*, "stretched"), and is, simply put, a specific verbal form that indicates the time an action took place, be it in relation to the moment of speech or in relation to another action. Throughout the world, verb tense ranges from the straightforward (future) to the strenuous (prehesternal past—something that happened the day before yesterday), and every new tense requires a subtle readjustment of your own internal space-time continuum.

Verb tense is often no less demanding for native speakers than it is for students. Some languages have literary verb tenses that are only used in print, having been dropped from colloquial usage. The French *passé simple* "*Je fis*," which is equivalent to the plain old English past tense (I did), today typically only shows up in writing. Spoken French uses a different—and easier—construction to mean the same thing: *J'ai fait* (literally "I have done"). In Serbo-Croatian, two past tenses have been largely relegated to writing on account of their specificity—each tense can only be used with certain verbs. As you might expect, then, in the spoken language, the preferred past tense is one that can be used with all verbs. Of course, the languages with the most literary tenses are the dead languages—which technically only have literary tenses.

Closely related to tense is something known as verbal aspect. Aspect isn't often discussed in English-grammar classes, in part because the English language conflates tense and aspect and in part because it's actually not so easy to explain. Frankly, most definitions of aspect give definitions a bad name. I have a Russian grammar book from 1962, for instance, that suggests looking to the lexical meaning of aspect: "the way a thing presents itself to the eye or mind." This is actually marginally better than what's in my other, newer Russian grammar, which doesn't really define aspect at all, choosing instead to go into a lengthy discussion about a man named Solomon who liked Belgian chocolates and walked with a limp.

I'm not deluded enough to think that I'll be able to succeed where legions of grammarians have failed, but I'm also just deluded enough to try. If you don't have the patience for slightly outlandish hypotheticals, I'd suggest skipping this paragraph. Imagine, for a moment, a time machine. With this time machine, you can spy on the actions of anyone, anywhere, anywhen. The moment in time that you travel to corresponds to tense; the status of the action when you get there corresponds to aspect. If the aspect is progressive or continuous, then, you'd see an ongoing action. If the aspect is imperfective, you'd see either an ongoing action or one that was habitually repeated. With perfect aspect, however, you'd see an action that had been completed but that still has some sort of relevance to the scene at hand. And a simple

Extraterrestrial Intelligence

Not all languages have tense or aspect—or even verbal inflection—but every language has verbs. Every language except one, that is. The Kēlen language is entirely without verbs, relying instead on four little words called "relationals" to link nouns together in a logical fashion. Kēlen is the creation of a woman by the name of Sylvia Sotomayor. While she was an undergrad in the linguistics department at Berkeley, she decided to take the language she had been working on for years and see what would happen if it were to violate one of the primary universals of human language. Unfortunately for verb-haters, the language is of little practical use: outside of constructed language enthusiasts, the only speakers of Kēlen are an alien race on the fictional planet Tērjemar.

aspect would just let you know that an action had, at some point, begun and ended.

The tricky thing about aspect is that, in many languages, tense and aspect aren't independent. A single verb "tense" is very often the combination of a tense *and* an aspect. It wasn't until I learned about aspect, for instance, that I really understood the French imperfect. And then it became so simple I would have burned my tattered old French book had I not already dumped it in the trash: the French imperfect is just a past tense with a progressive or repeated aspect, a trip back in time to catch somebody in the act.

Languages don't always, however, have the same combinations of tense and aspect. In English, a "perfect" verb always has the same aspect, no matter whether it's in the present (I have done), past (I had done), or future (I will have done) tense. In Latin, though, a past perfect verb can be either a past action with current consequences (as in English: past tense, perfect aspect) or a past action viewed as a single whole (past tense, simple aspect). *Fēcī*, then, can be translated into English either as "I have done" or as "I did."

A group of languages with a particularly sophisticated system of verbal aspect is the Slavic language family, which includes Russian, Ukrainian, Bulgarian, and Polish, among others. Slavic languages have two aspects, the perfective and imperfective, and most verbs come in pairs of each. Although this distinction does in some instances correspond to the complete and incomplete distinctions described above, very often the real meaning of Slavic aspect is significantly more complicated.

Take the Russian infinitive читать (*čitat'*)—"to read." *Čitat'* is an imperfective verb, which means that it can refer first and foremost to an ongoing action: one translation might be "to be reading." But in Russian, the imperfective can also refer to an action for which completion isn't really important, so sometimes *čitat'* could convey a sense not of reading like we would for a class, but like we would on vacation. Other times, the imperfective has a habitual sense, in which case you just have to imagine a parenthetical "as usual" after the verb.

When you elect to use the perfective form of the verb, which is created in this case by adding a prefix, "*pro-*" (прочитать, *pročitat'*), you're indicating completion or specificity. So the perfective form of the verb could be translated as "to read through (and finish)" or perhaps even "to read (that one time)."

Tense and aspect may be more complex than a flux capacitor, but when used correctly, they can provide a temporal specificity that even Doc Brown himself would envy.

VOICE AND MOOD
I think it's safe to say that of all the different ways

a verb can communicate meaning, the one that requires the least explanation for English-speakers is grammatical voice. Because if you've ever taken even the most elementary writing course—or come into contact with even the most elementary copyeditor—you've probably been inundated with grim warnings about the great evil of effective prose: passive voice.

Put most simply, when a verb is in the active voice, the subject performs the action; when a verb is in the passive voice, the subject is being acted upon. Passive constructions in English require the use of auxiliary verbs—typically a form of the verb "to be." Other languages, however, have special passive-voice verb forms. In Zulu, you can change an active verb to passive by changing a verb ending to -wa: *uyabona* "he sees"; *uyabonwa*, "he is seen." Japanese has two separate ways to express the passive voice, each of which has a slightly different meaning. The first form of the passive is translated exactly like the English passive voice. But the second form is only used when something kind of crappy and unexpected happens. Basically, if Alanis Morissette labeled it "ironic," then it would probably be expressed in the Japanese adversative passive. So if you got stuck in a traffic jam (when you're already late), you wouldn't say "I got stuck in traffic," you'd say something with a literal meaning closer to "I got stuck by the traffic." The implication being, of course, that it was all the traffic's fault.

Passive-Aggressives

Some languages have something called "deponent verbs." These verbs are like wolves in sheep's clothing: they may look like passive or middle verbs, but they have an active meaning. In Swedish, an easy way to make a verb passive is to add an *s*. But a few passive-looking verbs—*lyckas*, for instance, or *finnas*—actually have heartily active meanings: "to succeed" and "to exist." And in Latin, appropriately enough, a list of deponent verbs looks like a script for a deeply uncomfortable mother-daughter phone call: *hortor, mōlior, patior, morior*. I urge, I work at, I suffer, I die.

In Hausa, a language spoken by about forty million people throughout West Africa, active and passive verbs sometimes work much like their English counterparts. But other times, the relationship between subject and verb is much more literal than in English. An English passive verb, for instance, indicates that the action is directed at the subject. But in Hausa there's also a construction that indicates the literal direction of the action. If a verb ends in an -o and is spoken in a high tone (Hausa, like Mandarin, is a tonal language), then the action of the verb is physically directed toward the speaker. So the active-voice *shiga* means "to enter," and the passive-voice *shigo* means "to come in"—that is, to enter toward the speaker.

There are other voices as well, including reciprocal, reflexive, and—my own personal favorite—middle. I associate the middle voice with people who don't do things, but instead have them done, people like pop stars or mob bosses. Because when you use a verb in the middle voice, the result of the action is for the subject's own benefit. So if you put the beloved Ancient Greek sentence ἐπαίδευσα τοὺς νεανίας (*epaideusa tous neanias*)—"I educated the young men" into the middle voice, you have ἐπαιδευσάμην τοὺς νεανίας (*epaideusan tous neanias*). "I had the young men educated." Although presumably "I had the young men educated" would mean something very different if it were said by Tony Soprano—or, come to think of it, Aristotle.

As with so many other fine points of grammar, Sanskrit has found a pithy way to distinguish between the active and middle voices. In Sanskrit, the term for active voice, *parasmaipada*, means "word for another." The middle voice, however, is known as *ātmanepada*—"word for oneself."

Mood, on the other hand, can't be summed up so neatly. Grammatical mood is a tiny window into a person's perspective: it reveals something about the opinions, intentions, or hopes of the speaker. Mood does not, however, have anything to do with emotional mood, although it is nearly as wide-ranging. English has three moods; the first two are quite straightforward. The indicative, which is used for stating a fact or asking a question, is what we use the vast majority of the time. And the imperative is the command form of a verb—basically, anything you'd yell at a sporting event. The indicative and the imperative are the most basic verbal moods, which means that they tend to be a bit dry, grammar-wise. If moods were Baskin-Robbins ice-cream flavors, the indicative and imperative would be vanilla and French vanilla—one only slightly more interesting than the other.

The third English mood, however, is rather like Rocky Road. The subjunctive can connote all sorts of things: uncertainty, possibility, wishful thinking (which means, I suppose, that it might also often come up at sporting events). In many languages,

English included, the subjunctive is falling by the wayside, giving way to more intuitive indicative forms. Many Romance languages, however, still use the subjunctive extensively, not only in phrases expressing doubt, hope, or uncertainty as above, but also as a super-polite way to make requests. If you want to delicately tell somebody what to do in Italian, for instance, you wouldn't use the second-person imperative *scusa* (excuse me), but rather a third-person subjunctive *scusi* (excuse me—but only if it's not an inconvenience). English-speakers might recognize a similar construction used when making requests of the most respectful sort: asking things of god. If you've ever wondered why it's "God save the Queen" and not "God saves the Queen," well, now you know: it's the subjunctive. We're just trying to be polite.

A number of languages—including Ancient Greek, Japanese, and, in a last few traces, Persian— have what's called an optative mood. A close cousin of the subjunctive, the optative is used primarily for wishing and hoping, as in the Sanskrit *syāma*, "may we be." (In one of the more inexplicable quirks of English pronunciation, "optative" was pronounced op-TATE-ive by a British teacher of mine and OP-tat-tive by an American one. Later, I would ask a Russian grad student about the difference, and he would laugh at me.)

Some languages have a mood that's used solely for asking questions. If you need to ask a question in Venetian, a Romance language closely related to Italian (but distinct from the Italian Venetian dialect), you have to add an interrogative ending to the verb: "I finish" is *finiso*, but "do I finish?" is *finisoi*. Other languages, by the way, have special verb forms for answering questions. Welsh, for instance, doesn't have dedicated words for yes or no. If you want to answer a question in the affirmative, you often have to

---

Dawn of the Dead

Sanskrit is often lumped in with Latin and Greek, consigned to the dusty shelves of Languages Whose Time Has Passed. There is, however, an ongoing movement to reanimate Sanskrit and encourage its use as a modern-day tongue. And in some parts of the world, it's working. In the village of Mattur, which is located in the southern Indian state of Karnataka, most residents use Sanskrit daily, and children study the language from a very early age. Of course, for Sanskrit to be adapted for modern life, speakers have had to coin a number of new words, such as those for mobile phones, computers, and e-mail: *niṣṭantu dūravāṇī* (free-from wire distant voice), *gaṇakayantra* (enumerating apparatus), *vidyutsandeśa* (lightning message). My favorite word in modern Sanskrit, though, is undoubtedly the word for physics; *bhautaśāstra*. Which means, literally, "idiot science."

use an affirmative form of the verb *bod*, "to be." This can be a bit of a nuisance for learners, but I rather enjoy it. It gives even the most quotidian dialogues a thoroughly existential air:

Ydych chi'n hoffi te?	Do you like tea?
Ydw.	I am.
Ydych chi'n hoffi coffi?	Do you like coffee?
Nac ydw.	I am not.

Every language has a different set of moods to call its own. Some moods are self-explanatory (the presumptive, the declarative); some are not (the jussive, which is typically used to give commands or permission). In Albanian, the admirative mood is used to express surprise or wonder, as in a late-night infomercial: "Why, the Lean Mean Grilling Machine really *does* work!" In Latvian, a rather unusual mood called the debitive indicates the necessity of performing the action in question. This also seems well suited to salesmanship: instead of relying on the weak-willed indicative *tu pērc* "you buy," you can use the strong-armed debitive *tev jāpērk* "you must buy."

One of the most provocative moods is, in my opinion, the inferential, a mood used when the speaker is inferring something—in other words, when the speaker is talking about something that he or she didn't witness firsthand. In Turkish, there are two forms of the past, one in the definite past and one in the inferential past. If you use the definite past, the implication is that you have some sort of authority to be doing so—*gitti*: "He went (and I should know.)" The inferential past is a bit more like a shady bit of tabloid scandalmongering—*gitmiş*: "He went…*allegedly*." In my more contemplative moments, I like to imagine what havoc the inferential past could wreak on the celebrity news machine—much less the American political system.

IRREGULARITY AND IMPOSSIBILITY

For most of us, there's no dirtier word in language study than this one: irregular. Irregularities mean more work, more study, more missed questions on pop quizzes. Unfortunately, if a language has inflected verbs, it probably has more than a few irregularities—and English is no exception. Although English only has a few irregular verbs in the present tense, it has a ton of them in the past tense. I have yet to meet the English-speaker, native or otherwise, who hasn't struggled at some point with irregular English verbs. Because on the one hand, we have sing, sang, and sung. On the other hand, we have bring and brought. And that's only the beginning.

I myself remember being particularly confused about "brought" when I was a kid. I was about six years old by the time that my language had become sophisticated enough for me to start screwing up past participles, and I just couldn't get a handle on "brought." I kept saying "brung" instead. My parents tried admirably to explain to me why bring and sing were different, but I didn't get it. Eventually, they brought the lesson back around to my favorite thing: food and drink. "Do you eat bratwurst or brungwurst?" they would ask me, loudly and in public.

I got over my verbal slip-up soon thereafter.

But there's a reason for many of the irregular verb forms that we have in English—a reason beyond "that's just the way it is." Despite its relatively uninflected, freewheeling ways, English is still very much a Germanic language. Verbs in Old English are, as in modern German, classified as either "weak" or "strong." To form the past tense of a strong verb, you change the stem; to change the tense of a weak verb, you change the ending. So modern English verbs like "sing," which has managed to stick around since the days of Old English, when it was the strong verb *singan*, still follow that Old English strong-verb paradigm: sing, sang, sung. Verbs like "look," which derives from the weak verb *lōcian*, follow the simpler pattern of look, looked.

Old English had its own irregular verbs, though, like *sēcan*, "to seek," which had the past participle *sōht*. My childhood foe comes from the Old English *bringan*, which had the past participle *brōht*. Even though I still haven't managed to nail down the details of irregular English verbs with 100 percent precision ("lay" and "lie" will, I fear, always give me serious pause), I have figured one thing out: if there's some sort of whacked-out spelling like a silent "gh" in a verb, Old English is probably to blame.

Old English isn't the only language that has bequeathed to its progeny a legacy of verbal confusion and childhood humiliation. But some languages are surprising not for their irregularity, but for their regularity—like, for instance, Quechua (pronounced KETCH-wuh, not KWEE-cha as I mistakenly pronounced it for many years). Quechua was the primary language of the Inca empire and is still spoken throughout parts of South America—it's even an official language in Peru and Bolivia.

Although many indigenous South American languages are brutally complex, Quechua is different. First of all, it was a *lingua franca*, and as a general rule, the more people that speak a language, the less insanely difficult it is. Quechua was also chosen to be the language of the Inca empire. As Chimú, the language of the first Inca rulers, was incredibly difficult, I suspect that Quechua was singled out by the Early Inca Language Bureau for not being miserably impossible. But whatever its history, Quechua is extremely regular: nouns follow a single declension

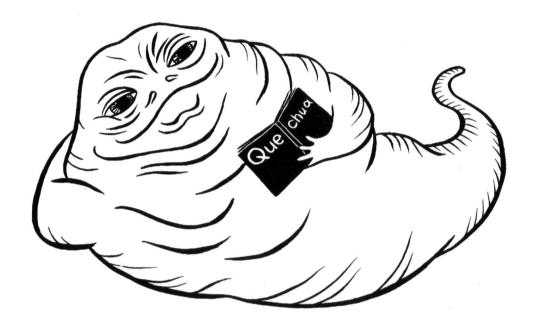

You May Have Been a Good Smuggler, but Now You're Bantha Fodder

----

The grammar of Huttese, the language spoken by Jabba the Hutt in the *Star Wars* movies, was closely modeled on Quechua. Much of the vocabulary, however, which includes words like *poodoo* (animal fodder) and *bunky dunko* (home), was not.

pattern, adjectives are invariable, and grammatical gender does not exist. The language also features a complete lack of irregular verbs: if you learn one verb conjugation, you've learned them all.

Take a Quechua infinitive, any infinitive. Then dump the last letter (all infinitives in Quechua end in "-y") and add the following endings to the verb:

	SINGULAR	PLURAL
1st	I -ni	We (inclusive) -nchis We (exclusive) -yku
2nd	You -nki	You -nkichis
3rd	He/She/It -n	They -nku

The lone peculiarity here appears in the first-person plural pronouns: the inclusive we means "we and you"; the exclusive we means "we and not you." But once you have this down, you can conjugate every Quechua verb in the present tense. So if you take *riy*, "to go," then "I go" is *rini*. If you take *khuyay*, "to love," then "they love" is *khuyanku*. And if you add *rqa* to the beginning of these endings, you can conjugate everything in the simple past tense: *rirqani*, "I went," *khuyarqanku*, "they loved."

Unfortunately, verbal regularity isn't the lone determinant of verbal simplicity. Navajo is the most widely spoken indigenous language in the United States, with close to 200,000 speakers. It is also famously, famously challenging. And not because it's chock-full of irregularities, but because its very structure is so damn complicated.

Navajo, which its speakers call *diné bizaad* ("words of the people"), is what's known as an "agglutinating" language, which means that words are formed by adding prefixes and suffixes to a base and building a big long mess of letters with a meaning that English would probably take a whole sentence to say. In some agglutinating languages, it's easy to pick out the affixes from the stems. Navajo has a nasty habit, however, of contracting everything so that the verb looks rather like a conjugation from linguistic hell.

To construct a verb in Navajo, the first thing you need to do is choose the proper verb stem. In most languages, finding a verb stem is as simple as opening up a dictionary. Not so in Navajo. First of all, any given meaning—"to give," perhaps—has a whole bunch of verb stems associated with it. And you have to choose wisely: not only does each stem have a different aspect, mood, and person associated with it, but some verbs also have to take into account the physical properties of the object. So you have to pick the right verb stem for the object that's being handled: there are stem endings for solid, roundish

Windtalking

The Navajo language was used to great effect in World War II as the basis for a military encryption system that was never cracked by the Japanese. The way it works is pretty cool: think about the modern military designations for letters like Bravo, Charlie, Tango, Quebec. The Navajo code was similar in that certain Navajo words stood for English letters—but only in the English translation. So the Navajo word *łįį'*, "horse," stood for H; *ł'ohchin*, "onion," stood for O; *tsitł'éli*, "matches," stood for M. When there wasn't time to spell out an entire message, shortcuts were developed. In some cases, Navajo words were used to substitute for frequent words. Sometimes the substitutions were straightforward (*dóone'é*, the Navajo word for "clan," stood for "corps"); sometimes the substitutions were less so (*ashįįh*, the Navajo word for "salt," stood for "division"). And then there are some phrases that aren't so much straightforward as shocking: the Navajo phrases used for China, Japan, and Africa were, respectively (and equally offensively), "braided hair," "slant eye," and "blackies."

objects (in the imperfective, -'aah), slender, stiff objects (-tįįh), open containers (-kaah), or my favorite, "mushy matter" (-tłeeh).

All in all, there are eleven main classificatory verb stems—which means that there are eleven different ways to say something as seemingly simple as "give it to me."

Next, you have to choose the correct prefix for your subject. There are four possible subjects in Navajo (first person, second person, and two distinct third persons) and three possible numbers (singular, dual, and plural), which means that there are twelve total possible person prefixes for each verb. They're not the same for every verb. And they're not the same for every tense. For instance, *yishcha* means "I cry," while *diskos* means "I cough." Even though these two verbs are the same in person, number, aspect, and mood, there's nothing in either to indicate that they might have anything in common.

Then, if you want to indicate a passive or a causative, you have to slip in *another* prefix before the stem. If the verb is transitive, you need to include an object prefix in there, too. And just in case that isn't enough for you, you can also choose to use a directional prefix—a prefix like *ná-*, perhaps, if you want to indicate repetition: *nihaa náádíídááł,* "Come see us again."

To be perfectly frank, if I were taking a class in Navajo, I'd be scared out of my mind. And prepping flash cards as if my life depended on it. Since I'm not taking a class, however, I can't help but be heartened. Because people do manage to learn Navajo. And Inuktitut. And Mapudungun. There are a great many testaments to the wondrous power of the human brain—philosophy, science, instant messaging. But of everything we've ever done, I am perhaps most impressed that we've managed to figure out the verb.

NUMBERS

One day, several thousand years ago, some prehistoric caveperson had the bright idea to keep track of sheep or moons or menstrual cycles by making a few marks on a bone. Ever since, humankind has come up with endless ways to deal with numbers. Some of us count with our hands. Some of us count with our feet.

We've used piles of pebbles, knots in a rope, beads on a wire. Some of us ignore higher numbers altogether, taking the same attitude toward numbers that I take toward the capital gains tax: if I don't need it, I don't need to know it.

Just as different cultures developed different technologies to record numbers, so languages have developed very different ways of expressing them. On an intuitive level, you might expect numbers to transcend cultural and linguistic boundaries. But in reality, the variation between number systems is nothing less than astonishing. Yes, it's true that five plus five always equals ten, but languages have dozens of different ways to express five and ten. If, in fact, they have numbers for five and ten at all.

NUMBER SYSTEMS

My most public linguistic accomplishment to date was when I, under the influence of nothing less than a kindergartner's utter lack of social grace, got up in front of a crowd and counted to fifty in French. To this day I consider it a small miracle that I managed to make it out of elementary school without being pummeled to death. At the time, though, I thought counting in another language was the coolest thing ever.

Had I gone past fifty, however, I might have felt very differently. Because the first fifty numbers in French are easy. You learn one through sixteen, twenty, thirty, forty, and fifty. Every other number is just a combination of these basic numbers: *vingt-et-un*, "twenty-and-one," *trente-neuf*, "thirty-nine."

But once you get past fifty, something strange happens. In English, numbers are really predictable. Stick a "-ty" after a number, and it probably means ten times that number: sixty, seventy, eighty. And in French, once you learn the first fifty numbers, you might expect something similar: instead of "-ty," though, you use "-*ante*": *quarante, cinqante*. Things get a little wonky at seventy, though. Seventy isn't *septante*, as you might expect, but *soixante-dix*, literally "sixty-ten." And eighty isn't *huitante*, but *quatre-vingt*, "four-twenty." As the French might say, *quel foutoir*.

Throughout history, humankind has been counting with groups. Some have historically counted in groups of five, some in groups of ten, and others in groups of twenty. The standard size of a counting group is what's known as a numerical base, and it varies from language to language—and sometimes, as with French, even within a language. In English, and in many, many other languages, the base is ten (also known as a decimal base). Large numbers, then, are combinations of groups of tens and ones: twenty equals two tens; fifty-five equals five tens plus five; a hundred and seven equals ten tens plus seven. And so forth. English has a particularly consistent number system, and all its numbers are based on a decimal reference. Even the two slightly irregular numbers eleven and twelve originally meant "one left" and "two left."

It doesn't take an evolutionary psychologist to figure out why base-10 is so popular—our most obvious accounting tools, after all, are our fingers. In many languages, number-words are even derived from words for fingers or hands. Many Zulu number-words, for instance, explicitly reference the number's associated hand gesture. The Zulu word for six is "*isithupa*," which literally means "extend the right thumb"—in addition, that is, to the five fingers on your left hand.

But base-10 isn't the be-all and end-all of number. Vigesimal systems (base-20) are not at all uncommon—a fact that isn't remotely surprising if you've ever bothered to add your fingers to your toes. The Maya, accomplished mathematicians and astronomers, are one of many people to rely on a vigesimal system: in Mayan, the number thirty-one is *buluc tu-kal*—literally, "eleven after the twentieth." Yuki, the language of a Native American people originally from northern California, has one of the world's more unusual numerical systems. The Yuki count with a base-8 system, the result of a tradition of counting with the *spaces between* the fingers.

A particularly intriguing counting tradition can be found in Yoruba, a language spoken primarily

To the Nines

A fun feature of Indo-European languages: the number nine is a heck of a lot like the word for "new."

Is this evidence of a long-ago change from base-8 to base-10, a sign that man started counting before he realized he had thumbs, or just the coincidental result of historical homophony? Probably the latter. But it's still a good bit of trivia.

	NINE	NEW		NINE	NEW
FRENCH	neuf	neuf	SWEDISH	nio	ny
SPANISH	nueve	nuevo	ICELANDIC	níu	nýr
ITALIAN	nove	nuovo	SANSKRIT	nava	nava
PORTUGUESE	nove	novo	LATIN	novem	novus
GERMAN	neu	neun	PERSIAN	noh	now
DUTCH	negen	nieuw	WELSH	naw	newydd
NORWEGIAN	ni	ny	IRISH	naoi	nua

in Nigeria, Benin, and Togo. The etymology of Yoruba counting relates not to human anatomy, but to the economy: many Yoruba number-words are derived from *owó*, the word for "cowrie shell," a standard unit of currency throughout large parts of Africa. When counting large quantities of shells, the Yoruba would count out five at a time and then group the shells into piles of ten, twenty, and two hundred. This method of counting is reflected in the traditional Yoruba number system, which reveals itself to be the quickest given way to count out a number from a table full of cowrie shells. To make the number 17, for instance, it's faster to deduct three shells from a pile of twenty than it is to take a pile of ten and count out an additional seven shells. So the traditional word for 17 isn't *ìdì l'èje*, "seven in addition to ten," but rather *èta dín logún*, "three removed from twenty."

As a result, Yoruba numbers tend to rely heavily on subtraction, much in the same way that time in English can be expressed as "a quarter to six" instead of "five forty-five"—except that it's used more often than not. The general rule with Yoruba numbers is this: if the unit's last digit is five or higher, you subtract from the next highest multiple of twenty. Yoruba only uses an English-style additive system for the first four numbers after any given unit of twenty. The word for eighty-seven, then, is *èta dín láàdórùn*, "three removed from ten removed from five twenties." It's a system that you'd rather be born into than have to learn, but it's clear that it did its job. After all, large commercial transactions often necessitated the counting of tens of thousands of shells. Even so, there is a movement in Yoruba toward switching to a base of *ìdì*—ten.

•   •   •

Although it's slightly depressing to think that such a rich and unusual number system would have to give way to base-10 banality, it's understandable, not just because of the need to standardize weights and measures and counting practices across cultural lines, but also because so many systems around the world use base-10. When you think about it, really, base-10 is a bit of a bully. It's been pushing other systems around for centuries.

As it turns out, though, sometimes the attempt to switch to a "simplified" decimal system results in a more complicated system overall. In Welsh, the result of the campaign to convert to a "modern" counting system has resulted in two distinct systems of numbers that you can use: one based on tens and one based on fifteens and twenties. So to say sixteen, you can either say *un deg chwech*, literally "one-ten-six," or you can say *un ar bymtheg*, "one on fifteen."

The Shepherd and His Flock

A lasting legacy of the Welsh number system can be found in a traditional vigesimal counting jargon that was once used throughout West Britain. Although the jargon was used primarily for the rather humdrum purpose of counting sheep, the words themselves are utterly charming, sounding like nothing so much as the names a young Will Shakespeare might have conjured up for a litter of adorable kittens: *yan, tan, tether, mether, pip, azer, sezar, akker, conter, dick, yanadick, tanadick, tetheradick, metheradick, bumfit, yanabum, tanabum, tetherabum, metherabum, jigget.*

And ninety-seven is either *naw deg saith*, "nine-ten-seven," or *dau ar bymtheg a phedwar ugain*, "two on fifteen and four twenties." The traditional counting system is used more often with casual speech, whereas the new system is used in schooling, but usage of either system varies widely—which is, to my mind, rather the opposite of standardization.

Many other modern base-10 systems also have the remnants of older vigesimal numbers. In Danish, the words for "fifty," "sixty," "seventy," "eighty," and "ninety" are all based on multiples of twenty. The Danish word for "seventy," for instance, is *halvfjerds*, which comes from a longer form *halvfjerdsindstyve*—literally, "four minus one half, times twenty." French, of course, has that troublesome *quatre-vingt*. And, thanks in no small part to a certain Civil War–era presidential address, English still has cause to make use of an alternative word for twenty: "score."

Even though the decimal system has the might of the many behind it, there are a few who actively advocate a move away from it—a move to, specifically, a duodecimal (or base-12) system. A base-12 system makes a great deal of arithmetical sense, given that twelve is a multiple of one, two, three, four, six, and twelve, so fractions like one-third and one-fourth of the base are whole numbers. This is surely one reason why units of twelve aren't uncommon in systems of measurement: if there are twelve inches to a foot, then a third of a foot is four whole inches. If there were only ten inches to a foot, though, a third of a foot would be the rather unwieldy three-and-one-third inches—or, in decimal notation, the even less wieldy 3.3333 ad infinitum. For simple, everyday arithmetic, a duodecimal base just makes things a bit neater.

But even though a base-12 system may be preferable in many respects, there are very few documented cases of duodecimal systems in the world's languages. The power of ten is hard to resist, whether you're a French scholar tasked with

Eats, Shoots & Counts
in Twelves

Because humans have ten fingers, it's no surprise that decimal systems rule the day. Imagine what might have happened, though, had another species risen to the top of the cognitive food chain. If three-toed sloths ruled the world, the dominant number system might be base-6; the four-toed hedgehog might have chosen base-8. And if pandas were in charge, they might have been lucky enough to stumble into base-12: pandas have six little panda fingers per paw. Which is why pandas are not only the mascots of punctuation sticklers everywhere, but also of a group of stateside advocates for a switch to base-12 living, the Dozenal Society of America.

inventing a new "metric" system of measurement or an Oxford don looking to flesh out a fantasy world. J. R. R. Tolkien, accomplished linguist and patron saint of the New Zealand economy, wrote in an appendix to *The Lord of the Rings* that his elves "preferred to reckon in sixes and twelves as much as possible." But Tolkien's duodecimal spirit seems to have sagged under the weight of decimal dominance—at least when it comes to laying out the specifics of his system. In part because elves, like humans, have ten fingers, Tolkien backed away from base-12 as he continued to construct the languages of Middle Earth. By the time of the Sindarin language, which I am told is the Elvish language of the "second age" (frankly, I got bored after *The Hobbit*), the system is unequivocally decimal:

canad	4
leben	5
pae	10
pae-a-canad	14 (10 and 4)
pae-a-leben	15 (10 and 5)

There is, however, evidence for the possible existence of a major duodecimal number system in Sumerian. The Sumerians were, as far as we know, the first culture to develop a written language, and this was due in no small part to a need to record commercial transactions, which also led to the development of symbols for numbers. (Which means that, I fear, there are a number of well-meaning archaeologists and linguists who are stuck spending their days deciphering the rough equivalent of, essentially, really old inventory lists.)

The Sumerian system is particularly noteworthy because although it featured a decimal system up to sixty, after that, it was hexagesimal—they used a base of *sixty*. With base-60, of course, you can get to some pretty big numbers pretty fast:

geš	60
geš-min	120 (60 x 2)
geš-u	600 (60 x 10)
geš-u-min	1,200 (60 x 10 x 2)

Sumerian even has words for *powers* of sixty—and if these words aren't convincing evidence of a culture used to dealing with huge numbers, I don't know what is:

šàr	3,600 (60 x 60)
šàrgal (literally, "big *šàr*") 2	216,000 (60 x 60 x 60)
šàrgal-šu-nu-tag (literally "bigger than big *šàr*")	12,960,000 (60 x 60 x 60 x 60)

No one knows why the Sumerians relied on a sexigesimal system—or indeed if it was even a conscious choice. But one possibility—posited by George Ifrah, the author of the gloriously comprehensive *The Universal History of Numbers*—is that the Sumerian system was the result of the intermingling of two separate number systems, one decimal, one duodecimal, and a base of sixty was chosen because sixty is the lowest common multiple of the two. It's also possible that it was chosen because of its many factors; because sixty happens to be a factor of 360, a rough approximation of the number of days in a year; or because it had some sort of spiritual relevance.

Whatever the reason, the Sumerian sexagesimal system is still with us today. The Sumerians were particularly skilled astronomers and geometers whose work was studied by Greek and Arabic scholars—and whose number system was adopted in the study of those disciplines. As a result, we can thank Sumerian for the division of a circle into 360 degrees, the division of an hour into 60 minutes, and the division of a minute into 60 seconds—something that not even the most gung-ho advocates of the metric system have been able to change.

NUMBERS AND NOUNS

There may be enough diversity in the world's number-words to fill more than a few doctoral dissertations, but number systems are just the tip of the linguistic iceberg. Different languages also have a wide and occasionally surprising variety of rules and structures that come into play once number-words are paired up with nouns. In some Semitic languages, number-words are governed by something called "reverse polarity." In both Hebrew and Arabic, the numbers three through ten take the *opposite* gender of the nouns they modify, a possible historical remnant of an earlier system in which Semitic plurals took the opposite of their original gender. If you want to say "three daughters" in Hebrew, then, you have to use the masculine form of the number "three": *shalosh banot*. And if you want to say "three sons," you have to use the feminine form: *shlosha banim*.

One of the more complicated systems of cardinal number–noun agreement occurs in Icelandic, which declines the numbers one through four not only for

Character Study

In Chinese, some characters use visual repetition to form plurals, one of the few instances in which Chinese characters mean something like they look.

木	mù	tree	林	lín	forest
石	shí	rock	磊	lěi	pile of stones
口	kǒu	mouth	品	pǐn	group of people

case and gender, but also for *number*. Icelandic makes a distinction between items that you would count individually and items that you'd count as a group—like a pair of skates, for instance, or a barbershop quartet. And when counting these groups in Icelandic, you need to use the plural form of the numbers one, two, three, or four. So while *tveir sokkar* means "two socks," *tvennir sokkar* means "two pairs of socks." This is, of course, a little surprising; you'd think that if anything in language were self-evident, it would be the number of a number. But I suppose I shouldn't be shocked that the same country that gave birth to Björk has more than one radical linguistic idiosyncrasy.

Many languages require the use of something called a "noun classifier" or "measure word." In English, the only nouns that take measure words are mass nouns—something like flour, for instance, which we measure in cups or bags or pounds because counting each grain is quite clearly deranged. In some languages, however, even nouns for things that might seem to be countable require the use of classifiers. And very often these classifiers will be linked to specific types of nouns, just as, in English, a "bottle" cannot be used to measure bread, and a "loaf" cannot be used to measure beer.

In Thai, there are, among others, classifiers for books, for people, and for generic nouns. And when you want to combine a number with a noun, you have to use a specific word order: noun, number, classifier.

nangsue sam lem	three books
dek sam khon	three boys
buri sam muah	three cigarettes

A language with a particularly diverse (and often, for foreign learners, infamous) set of classifiers is Mandarin. In Mandarin, with very few exceptions, whenever you use a cardinal number with a noun, you have to put a classifier between the numeral and the noun. The most common classifier is 个 (*gè*), which can be used with most kinds of nouns and is almost always used with people.

三个人	*sān gè rén*	three people
一个菜单	*yī gè càidān*	one menu

Gè is tempting as a catch-all classifier. When I was studying Mandarin, I'd usually just throw it in whenever I wasn't sure of the measure word—something that, along with the nonstandard accent I picked up in China, once caused a teacher to ask me why I was speaking like an illiterate peasant girl. Classifiers in Mandarin are very specific, however, and if you use the wrong classifier, you risk sounding like you just asked for "three cups of children."

Just as Thai has different classifiers associated with books, boys, and cigarettes, so too does Mandarin use different noun classifiers depending on the type of object, the shape of the object, or sometimes even an action that's associated with the object. Books and magazines, for instance, take the classifier 本 (*běn*):

五本书	*wǔ běn shū*	five books
七本杂志	*qī běn zázhì*	seven magazines

Whereas 条 (*tiáo*) is used for items that are, for lack of a better word, long and winding:

三条河	*sān tiáo hé*	three rivers
十条蛇	*shí tiáo shé*	ten snakes

Tools or implements often take the classifier 把 (*bǎ*), a word that can mean "to handle":

四把刀	*sì bǎ dāo*	four knives
一把梳子	*yī bǎ shūzi*	one comb

"Chair," inexplicably, is also included in this group:

九把椅子	*jiŭ bă yĭzi*	nine chairs

Korean and Japanese also use noun classifiers. But in these languages, you have to be aware of both the noun you're counting and the number you're using to count with. As with Latin and Arabic, political and economic might gave (and continues to give) Chinese some serious cultural cachet, and Japanese and Korean have been considerably influenced by the Chinese language. As a result, each language features two separate number systems, one native and one Chinese.

When counting in Korean from one to one hundred, you can take your pick from either set of numbers. Most of the time, however, you can only use a given noun classifier with one set of numbers or the other. And in the instances when a classifier can be used with both systems, the meaning of the classifier can change depending on which number set is chosen. For instance, if you use the classifier 분 (*bun*) with the Korean number "one," 하나 (*hana*), you get 한분 (*hanbun*), "one esteemed person." But if you use *bun* with 일 (*il*), the borrowed Chinese number for "one," the meaning changes to "one minute."

Japanese is a little bit simpler—at least in its spoken form. In Japanese, the traditional number system is only used for the numbers one through ten, and in the vast majority of situations, you can only use noun classifiers with the Chinese number system.

	ORIGINAL JAPANESE FORM	CHINESE LOAN FORM
1	ひとつ hitotsu	一 ichi
2	ふたつ futatsu	二 ni
3	みっつ mittsu	三 san
4	よっつ yottsu	四 yon
5	いっつ itsutsu	五 go
6	むっつ muttsu	六 roku
7	ななつ nanatsu	七 nana
8	やっつ yattsu	八 hachi
9	ここのつ kokonotsu	九 kyū
10	とお tō	十 jū

If you've studied Chinese, though, classifiers in the Japanese written language can be a bit more complicated. Japanese uses Chinese script much more frequently than does Korean, which creates a real problem: false friends. When two languages intermingle, oftentimes one language will borrow a word from another language. Sometimes, though, the meaning of the loan word will turn out to be slightly different from the meaning of the original, even if the two words sound like cognates. It's an irksome state of affairs for language learners—not to mention embarrassing. A typical example of a false friend is the Italian word *preservativo*, which sounds so similar to the English word *preservative*

Poetic License

As if two number systems weren't already enough, Japanese offers a third option for your everyday counting needs—in the form of poetry.

This is the first line of the Iroha, a centuries-old poem that contains each Japanese syllable once and only once and serves as an occasional stand-in for regular old numbers—a highbrow literary take, if you will, on eenie, meenie, miney, moe.

い	ろ	は	に	ほ	へ	と
i	ro	ha	ni	ho	he	to
1	2	3	4	5	6	7

BITING THE WAX TADPOLE

that you might assume it means "jam." Unfortunately for English-speakers (but hilariously for Italian-speakers), it actually means "condom."

Because Japanese script is based on Chinese characters, sometimes a character will show up in written Japanese that might look perfectly familiar to a speaker of Chinese and yet have an entirely unfamiliar meaning. If you don't think this seems like such a big deal, well, let me give you a hypothetical. Let's just say—hypothetically—that you worked your ass off for three years trying to memorize Chinese characters. You read about radicals and logograms and stroke order, and eventually you tricked your brain into being able to memorize symbols that are significantly more complicated than the Times New Roman character set. Then you get the silly idea that you might want to learn Japanese, too. It'll be easy, you think—you've already mastered the hardest part, which is learning how to look up the damned characters in a dictionary. And maybe there will be sushi involved.

And then you see something like this: 五本ペン. Great, you think—those first two characters are Chinese, so even though you don't yet know those other two symbols, an educated guess might be "five bound things"—maybe not books exactly, but brochures, perhaps, or some sort of technologically advanced Japanese presentation binders.

And you would be very wrong. Because the phrase means "five pens." In Japanese, 本 (*hon*) has two uses: either as the word for "book" itself, which makes some kind of sense if you've studied Chinese, or as a classifier for long, thin objects like pens and pencils—which makes no kind of sense if you've studied Chinese. I'm sure that reasonably fluent Chinese-readers have a real comparative advantage when studying Japanese script. Moderately crappy Chinese-readers like myself, however, are more or less screwed.

To make a long story short, number-words and classifiers aren't just an especially interesting aspect of grammar—they're also the reason I long ago swore off Japanese.

WRITTEN NUMBERS

In 1960, a Belgian explorer named Jean de Heinzelin de Braucourt was in what is today known as the Democratic Republic of Congo (and has variously been known as the Belgian Congo, Zaire, and The Congo) when he stumbled upon a dirty old monkey bone that turned out to be one of the earliest extant examples of written number-keeping. The Ishango bone, as it is known, is inscribed with a series of notches that may indicate the human ability not only to scratch out tally marks, but also to perform simple arithmetic.

The earliest evidence of a written language, however, comes courtesy of the Sumerians, who figured out that they could keep records by sticking a stylus into damp clay, a system of writing that we know today as *cuneiform* (from the Latin for "wedge"). Just to give you some chronological perspective on this, cuneiform is about five thousand years old. The Ishango bone, however, is believed to be more than twenty thousand years old. Keeping track of words is a relatively recent human invention, but we've been keeping track of numbers for tens of thousands of years. And even though Arabic numbers are predominant today, they've only been widely used for a few centuries, which means that written number systems have had a good many millennia to build up a bit of regional variation.

That being said, the first methods of accounting were typically just fancy tally marks, the shapes of which were largely determined by whatever passed for paper and pencil at the time. As such, even though the world's number systems vary widely, many of the world's most archaic ways of writing numbers look remarkably similar. The Sumerians, as I mentioned, recorded number by using a stylus to mark clay tablets: if the stylus was pressed in straight, it would make a dot, which was used as a symbol for "ten." If the stylus was held at an angle, though, it would make a little notch, which was used as the symbol for "one." The Maya and the Olmec both expressed numbers with symbols that aren't hugely dissimilar: a circle was used for ones, and a line was used for fives. And

Tally-ho

In many countries in Asia, the Chinese character 正 (*zhèng*) is used as a tally mark in lieu of the traditional "five-barred gate." To draw the character yourself (or to interpret it when you see it on a receipt at a Chinese restaurant), start by drawing the top horizontal stroke. Then, draw your second stroke down, making a T. Next, draw the middle line to make a funny-looking F. Finally, draw the left-hand vertical stroke and wrap it up with a nice decisive line at the bottom.

in ancient China, horizontal lines were scratched on oracle bones to mark the numbers one through four, while a vertical line indicated units of ten.

For all the subtlety and sophistication of Egyptian hieroglyphs, the basic written numbers of ancient Egypt weren't much more complex than any other ancient number system. Egyptians represented powers of ten with the symbol ∩ and powers of one with our old tally-mark friend, the vertical line. And, as with the above systems, higher numbers were created with repetition. To form the numbers one through one hundred in Egyptian, all you have to do is provide the appropriate number of ones and tens: 41 = | ∩∩∩∩.

An ancient number system still in use today, no doubt due to its smug Latinate affiliation, is the Roman numeral system. The Roman numeral system did not, however, emerge fully formed from the head of some forward-thinking poet who figured that one day a bunch of crappy Hollywood sequels would need a way to class up their titles. Nor did it derive, as many might think, from Latin number-words (M for *mille*, "thousand," for example). The origins of the Roman system are actually the same as those of the Egyptian, Sumerian, and even prehistoric Congolese systems: the tally mark.

Think about scratching a tally mark into the side of, say, a dank prison cell. The easiest mark to make is a straight line. If you want to have a system, chances are you're going to use some combination of vertical lines, horizontal lines, and angled lines. So it's perfectly natural that you'd end up with a series of symbols that probably include signs that look something like I, V, and X. Roman numerals aren't particularly majestic or innovative; they're just the result of yet another group of people scratching things to keep count.

It took a long, long time for humans to really improve on the notches found on the Ishango bone. The first big technological breakthrough in number technology came with the invention of the alphabet, which allowed for the creation of "ciphers" in which the first letter of a number-word could stand for the number itself. In the Ancient Greek number system, Δ stood for "ten" (ΔÉKA, *deka*), and M stood for "ten thousand" (MÝRIOI, *myrioi*).

Soon thereafter, however, some clever Greek realized that each letter of the alphabet could be assigned a number: α (alpha) = one, β (beta) = two, γ (gamma) = three, ι (iota) = ten, ρ (rho) = one hundred. One hundred and twelve, then, could be easily expressed as ριγ, 100 + 10 + 2. I suppose I should point out that it's also possible that some clever Greek realized that Hebrew had used this system first and borrowed it. But whoever thought of it first, the point is that the alphabetic system was, at the time, the Cadillac of number systems, and its use spread far beyond the shores of Greece. Alphabetic number systems show up in the traditional number systems used by Gothic, Georgian, Armenian, and just about any language that adopted the Cyrillic alphabet. Even Arabic at one point used a similar number system. Some cultures just adopted the Greek alphabet wholesale—albeit as a number system. If you look at the traditional number system of Ge'ez, the ancient language of Ethiopia and Eritrea, you'll find an only slightly reworked version of the Greek alphabet.

The Greek alphabetic system is still sometimes used today in much the same self-conscious way that Roman numbers are used, and the Hebrew alphabetic

---

The Mark of the Beast

Ever since the Book of Revelation declared that the Number of the Beast was "six hundred threescore and six," numerologists and religious scholars have been in a frenzy to identify the marked man, convinced that 666 was meant as an alphabetic cipher. Some suggest that it pointed to Nero, the Roman emperor whose rule coincides with many estimates of the date of the book's creation. If you loosely transcribe Nero's name into Hebrew, you get *nrwn qsr*, or 50 + 200 + 6 + 50 + 100 + 60 + 200 = 666. Others prefer to turn to Greek, identifying Λατεῖνος (*lateinos*), "Latin-speaker," as a possible solution: 30 + 1 + 300 + 5 + 10 + 50 + 70 + 200 = 666. Whether this is meant to implicate the Roman Empire or the Roman Catholic Church, I couldn't say. Latin itself presents a number of intriguing possibilities, including my favorite, posited by the unfortunately named Catholic mystic Petrus Bungus: LVTHERNVC = 30 + 200 + 100 + 8 + 5 + 80 + 40 + 200 + 3 = 666. Because, as any good sixteenth-century Catholic knew, there was no man so beastly as Martin Luther.

BITING THE WAX TADPOLE

system continues to be extremely important for certain branches of Jewish mysticism. But no number system has the modern-day relevance of the numbers popularly—but not entirely accurately—known as "Arabic numbers." Although the Italian mathematician Fibonacci, who is widely credited with popularizing the system in Europe, first learned the number system while living in North Africa, the origin of the symbols actually lies farther to the east—in India. (Which is why you've probably heard the term "Hindu-Arabic numerals" bandied about.)

Today, the vast majority of the world's people have adopted Hindu-Arabic numerals, a useful turn of events if you happen to be a tourist looking for an address abroad or a mathematician seeking world dominance. Even so, I can't help but think that arithmetic would be significantly more enjoyable if we still made use of hash-marked monkey bones.

THE MEANING OF NUMBER

Some languages account very minimally for number. Take, for example, Warlpiri, an aboriginal language concentrated not far from Alice Springs in Australia's Northern Territory. Although Warlpiri has relatively complex systems of verb conjugation and noun derivation, its number system lacks the higher-order cardinal numbers found in many other languages and relies instead on a distinction between one, two, and many. Or there's Pirahã, an Amazonian language quixotic enough to have inspired at least one *New Yorker* article and much gnashing of teeth among linguists. According to Daniel Everett, a linguist and ex-missionary who has studied the language for decades, although the word *hói* (with a high tone on the "o" and a low tone on the "i") can be translated as "one," it more accurately means "small size or amount." Meanwhile, the word *hoí* (with a low tone on the "o" and a high tone on the "i") can mean "slightly larger size or amount." Pirahã doesn't "just" have a one-two-many system—it has no numbers at all.

So how do the Pirahã count? They don't. And here's the thing: they don't have to. Counting isn't a science, it's a technology—it's something created in response to a given need. Yoruba society depended on the counting of huge numbers of shells; the Yoruba number system reflects that. Some cultures, though—the Warlpiri or the Pirahã—have no reason to count huge numbers of shells. Pirahã is a particularly isolated language with a barter-based economy and incredibly complex cultural notions of immediacy, neither of which lends itself well to notions of number. For the Pirahã, there simply hasn't historically been a need for counting, and the language and culture reflect that.

There's nothing smart or stupid about any one number system. Some work better than others with large numbers or with fractions. In the modern intellectual tradition, numbers are the new Virgin Mary: pure, unassailable, and even a bit magical. Statistics and mathematics transcend cultural boundaries, so it might be tempting to use numbers as a way to compare one language—or one people— to another. Avoid the temptation. Number systems, are, like language itself, cultural artifacts, the unique results of a series of what are, essentially, historical accidents.

MODIFIERS

In the nineteenth century, "the Adjective" wasn't just a phrase used by grimly determined tutors or in humorless grammatical tomes. It also served as a euphemism for a delightfully multipurpose—and at the time extremely risqué—modifier: "bloody." Today the word is so commonplace that it rarely inspires much more than an occasionally raised eyebrow, but in the early days of its usage, "bloody" was considered to be an affront to polite society. In 1914, Eliza Doolittle's theatrical exclamation of "Not bloody likely" inspired countless criticisms on both sides of the Atlantic—a *New York Times* article ("Shaw's Adjective Shocks") noted that the then-Bishop of Woolwich believed that the word should simply be banned. And for all those Europeans who tease Americans about their puritanical ways, I might mention that "bloody" still causes the occasional kerfuffle across the pond. As recently as 2006, broadcasting regulators in the UK tried to force an Australian tourism campaign ("So where the bloody hell are you?") to clean up its language.

There are various theories as to the origin of the word—a variation of "by Our Lady," a reference to the blood of Jesus Christ, evidence of the patriarchy's continued distrust of female biology—but whatever its etymology, there's no doubt that "bloody" is up there with "knickers," "wanker," and "mum" as one of the more characteristic bits of British English.

"Bloody" is, of course, even more beloved by the Australians, who have long since adapted the word for use in very nearly any situation—as ably demonstrated in W. T. Goodge's brilliant poem "Bloody! (The Great Australian Adjective)," which culminates thusly:

He plunged into the bloody creek,
The bloody horse was bloody weak,
  The stockman's face a bloody study!
And though the bloody horse was
drowned
The bloody rider reached the ground
  Ejaculating, "Bloody!"
     "Bloody!"

It should be noted that in early printings, the adjective in question was replaced with a series of unerringly polite dashes.

Nouns, verbs, and numbers are all well and good if you want to scrape by with a bare minimum of language. But if you want to do anything really fun, if you want to tell a great story, offend a strait-laced regulator, or tell off your best friend's lousy ex-boyfriend, then modifiers, bloody and otherwise, are your ticket.

ADJECTIVES

Even though the grammar of adjectives might not be quite as compelling as the history of the Adjective, it is nonetheless surprisingly colorful. Adjectives can act as attributes: pretty horses, purple haze, Old English. Or they can take a more emphatic role as

The Color of Money

In 1960, a book was written in response to a bet: write a children's book with only fifty words. Among those fifty words were some hardworking nouns and verbs and a handful of prepositions and conjunctions. But the single most important word was a modifier: green. With a single adjective, Theodor Geisel was able to take an otherwise unexceptional pair of breakfast foods and turn them into literary fodder for generations. And his editor was able to take a $50 bet and turn it into a hell of a lot more.

predicatives: the hills are alive, this house is clean. Most of the time, the order of nouns and attributive adjectives in a language is fixed. In English, adjectives always come before the noun: green eggs, green ham. In Spanish, on the other hand, adjectives very often come after the noun: *huevos verdes, jamón verde*. Although the vast majority of French adjectives come after the noun, there are a few that can precede it. (Which, if you're interested, you can remember with the mnemonic BAGS: beauty, age, goodness, size.) So although you would say *la crème anglaise*, you would never say *le prince petit*.

In Tibetan, the order of nouns and adjectives depends on the type of adjective. Although adjectives usually come after the noun (*kah-lah trahng-mo*, "cold food"), when a proper noun is used as an adjective, it's placed before the noun: *Phö-beh kah-lah*, "Tibetan food." And in some languages, the placement of the adjective can affect its meaning: in Spanish, *un hombre grande* means "a big man," but *un grande hombre* means "a great man."

Many languages have different rules for attributive and predicative adjectives. Some Czech adjectives have short forms that can only be used in the predicate, such as *rád*, "glad," and *zdráv*, "healthy." The Sámi languages of Scandinavia and Russia, from which we get the English word "tundra," have separate forms for attributive and predicative adjectives. In Inari Sámi, *kiergâðis* (fast) can describe a "fast wolf" or "fast wolves." If you want to use the adjective in the predicate, however, you have to use the forms *kiergâd* or *kiergâðeh*, as in *kuumpih láá kiergâðeh* "the wolves are fast."

German adjectives, like German verbs, come in weak and strong varieties. As a further complication, some German adjectives also have a third form, known as "mixed." So for each German adjective, you're looking at twelve possible singular and plural forms, depending on the type of determiner that's attached:

	WEAK	MIXED	STRONG
	"the good book"	"a good book"	"good book"
NOM.	das gute Buch	ein gutes Buch	gutes Buch
ACC.	das gute Buch	ein gutes Buch	gutes Buch
GEN.	des guten Buches	eines guten Buches	guten Buches
DAT.	dem guten Buch	einem guten Buch	gutem Buch

Please note that this is a common paradigm in German grammars and not at all an attempt at any sort of subconscious manipulation.

Strong and weak adjectives are widespread throughout Germanic languages: some form of the system can be found in Norwegian, Icelandic, and Danish. You can even still find it in Dutch, a language that is otherwise pretty much a cakewalk for English-speakers. Whenever I'm feeling particularly downtrodden about my language skills, flipping through a Dutch grammar always helps brighten my mood. Although, to be fair, this might also have something to do with the fact that my favorite Dutch grammar is structured around the adventures of Baron von Münchhausen—or in Dutch, Baron *van* Münchhausen.

Dutch adjectives have two forms: they either take an "e" on the end or they don't. The e-form is used for all attributive adjectives, with two exceptions. If the noun is a neuter singular and isn't modified by a definite article, then the adjective is uninflected. So "a good beer" is *een goed bier*. To say "the good beer," on the other hand, you need to use an e-form adjective: *het goede bier*. An e-free adjective can also signal that the modifier is being used in a less-than-literal way, as in *een grote mens*, "a big man," and *een groot mens* "a great man"—the difference between "big" and "great" apparently being a central concern of adjectives everywhere.

We learn in school that nouns and adjectives are separate parts of speech, but in many languages, including English, nouns and adjectives have a tendency to intermingle. Sometimes words that are usually adjectives can also be used as nouns (the

The Brothers Grimm

The terms "strong" and "weak" as used in grammar were originally coined by Jacob Grimm, the linguist and scholar responsible for several important works on German grammar and historical linguistics. His most lasting contribution to the field of linguistics is "Grimm's Law," a systematic pattern for the evolution of sounds in language. Despite his impressive academic achievements, however, Grimm is best known not for his linguistics work, but rather for his interests in folklore and mythology. And for the fact that he, along with his brother Wilhelm, is at least partially responsible for something far scarier than Cinderella's wicked stepmother: Disney.

bold and the beautiful, the young and the restless); other times, words that are usually nouns can be used as adjectives (soap opera). Of course, you can also derive adjectives from nouns (child, childlike, childish), and in a number of languages, you don't have to do anything to the form of a word to make it a candidate for dual noun-adjective citizenship. Oftentimes, the difference between a noun and an adjective depends not so much on what a given word means, but rather on its context. It's all very European Union: there's free movement everywhere.

In Hausa there's no lexical distinction at all between adjectives and nouns. But you can't just slap two nouns together and hope that they manage to make sense—nor can you do the same with a descriptive noun compound. Linking two Hausa nouns requires something called the "construct state," in which the first noun in the chain is marked with an -*n* or an -*ř*, a grammatical signal that the nouns are coupled. The same structure is used when one noun modifies another in an adjective-like way. As a result, literal translations of Hausa can sound particularly roundabout to English-speakers: *farař saaniyaa,* "white cow," more literally means something like "cow-with-whiteness."

A similar phenomenon is found in Persian and Kurdish. When Persian or Kurdish adjectives are placed after the nouns they modify (as they almost always are, except in poetry), a special ending known as an *ezāfe* has to be added to the noun. The Persian *ezāfe* is pretty simple to learn. First, take a look at the noun. If it ends in a consonant or an *-i*, add an *-e*; otherwise, add a *-ye*. To modify *ketāb*, "book," you would add an *-e*: *ketābe khub*, "the good book." And if you want to use more than one adjective with your noun, then add an *ezāfe* to the first adjective as well: *sage siyāhe gonde*, "the big black dog." The *ezāfe* can be used to link two nouns, to link a noun and an adjective, or, as above, to link multiple adjectives to a noun. The *ezāfe* is a territory marker, plain and simple: the following word belongs to me.

In other languages, adjectives behave like verbs. To sign "you are beautiful" in American Sign Language, you would simply make the sign for "you" and then the sign for "beautiful." In ASL, the verbal and adjectival functions are contained within a single sign—a better translation of the sign, then, might be "is beautiful."

Mandarin adjectives behave similarly: all Mandarin adjectives have a verbal component. If you were to run the Mandarin word 美丽 (*měilì*) through an online translator, you'd probably get a definition of "beautiful." But 美丽 (*měilì*) doesn't have the same grammatical function as its English translation—it doesn't require a "to be" verb between a noun and an adjective. As with ASL, all the juicy verbal action is wrapped up in the adjective itself. So "she is beautiful" is simply 她美丽 (*tā měilì*), literally "she beautiful." As attributives, things are a little bit more complicated: to pair an adjective with a noun, you have to add the particle 的 (de): 这个美丽的女孩子 (zhèige měilì de nǚháizi) means "the beautiful girl," but might be more precisely translated as "the being-beautiful girl."

This is, I suspect, one reason why many Chinese-to-English translations seem so clumsy—sometimes they're not incorrect so much as hypercorrect. I can't help but think of my favorite toy when I was a kid, a small, battery-operated convertible that my parents brought me back from Beijing. There were two figures in the front seats, and in the arms of the passenger was a tiny, old-fashioned press camera. When you turned it on, the car drove in circles and the flash bulb went off periodically. The name of the toy? The Photoing-On Car.

COLORS

Anyone who has ever had the unpleasant task of picking out a paint color is well acquainted with the absurdity of color naming. You can't go in with a simple preference for brown or purple. Instead you're going to have to choose between ochres, siennas, and umbers; violets, lavenders, and aubergines. If you're really unlucky you'll find yourself confronted with words that may or may not be remotely related to the color of the paint in question: Checkerberry, Alakazam, Timothy Straw, Tunnel of Love. (By the way, that last color is, inexplicably, a rather nondescript gray.)

Color in language is no less complicated—but for very different reasons. The first time I cracked open a guide to Shona, a Bantu language spoken primarily in Zimbabwe, I was rather taken aback when I reached the section on color. The author listed words for red, black, white, brown, yellow, and gray, but there was no word for green. Nor was there a word for blue. At first, I figured that I'd somehow managed to pick up a less-than-accurate grammar. (It wouldn't have been the first time.) But after a bit of digging around, I discovered that in one dialect of Shona, there aren't separate words for blue and green. Instead, blue and green are grouped together under the word *pfumbu*— which in my book was literally translated as "gray."

I was flummoxed. Color is one of the very first things that I can ever recall liking or disliking. As a child, I constructed my entire identity around the fact that I was the kind of girl who preferred blue and green to pink and purple. Blue and green were so important to me that I even made an attempt to cover our two-story stucco house in a layer of blue and green crayon. (Luckily for my mother, my five-year-old attention span stopped me before I got too far.) So the idea of not having words for blue and green wasn't hard for me to grasp just on a linguistic level,

A Color By Any Other Name

Blood and water (and, grotesquely, bile) are frequent referents of basic color terms, but the origin of many color terms isn't always so fluid-fixated. The Mandarin word for gray, 灰色 (*huīsè*), translates as "ash-colored." The Persian word *khāk*, which means "dust," has found its way both into the English language and the wardrobe of investment bankers everywhere. In Yele, one of the many languages of Papua New Guinea, the word for white—*kpaapîkpaapî*—is just the reduplicated name of a species of white cockatoo. And ʔilp'ilp, the word for red in Nez Percé, a nearly extinct Native American language, is perhaps most evocative: it's derived from the word for pimple.

BITING THE WAX TADPOLE

but on a basic emotional level as well. As it turns out, though, languages didn't evolve with the express intention of affirming the psychological validity of my childhood experience. And Shona is far from the only language that relies on a system of basic colors that is different from the one I grew up with.

The most basic color distinction found in language is between dark and light. On the island of New Guinea, a region with hundreds of known living languages, a number of people get by with only two basic color terms: "white" and "black." Contrary to some early and outlandish anthropological theories, this does not mean that the native speakers of these languages only see black and white. It just means that in these languages, every color in the visual spectrum is assigned one color-term or the other. And it's not always intuitive which colors count as white and which count as black. In one of the Dani languages, spoken on the Indonesian half of the island, red, which I usually think of as a rich, deep color, is classed as *mola*, "white," whereas green, which I for some reason associate most closely with AstroTurf, is *muli*, "black."

Nor does a relative paucity in basic color terms mean that a language can't find other ways to express subtle variations in color. In their landmark work on the evolution of color terms in language, Brent Berlin and Paul Kay pointed out a study of Paliyan, a dialect of Tamil spoken in southern India, which revealed that although the language uses light and dark to differentiate between colors, it uses five separate terms to communicate degrees of brightness: *ve̠lle* ("illuminated"), *manja* ("bright"), *nīlam* ("of medium brightness"), *sihappu* ("dark"), and *karuppu* ("in shadow"). On the other side of the world is a group of languages that use compound terms to expand and refine their color systems. Most Mayan languages feature only five basic color terms, typically some variation of *ʔik'* (black), *sak*, (white), *čak* (red), *k'an* (yellow), and *yaš* (blue-green). When a more precise color-word is needed, though, these terms can be combined with other words to indicate nuances in intensity, in opacity, in texture. For instance, in Yucatek Maya, a language of both the Yucatan and the chosen tongue of Mel Gibson's *Apocalypto*, the color *k'an* can be combined with *hep'* (a word meaning "tighten" or "squeeze") to communicate "deep yellow." This system of color-compounding is so widespread and productive that in Tzotzil, a related Mayan language, there are nearly one thousand possible color compounds, all based on those five basic color terms.

• • •

All the same, because we learn color words at such a young age, it can take some time to adjust to variations in color systems. Consider again those two troublesome colors in Shona, blue and green.

Rhymes With Orange

In many languages, the word for orange is relatively new. So new, in fact, that lots of languages got their words from the same place—which means that throughout the world, there are surprisingly few words for orange. The first set of words—including the English version—derives from *nārang*, the Persian name for the bitter orange fruit originally native to Southeast Asia. Some of these languages actually use a word derived from *nārang* for the color, but another word for the fruit. In Dutch, the color orange is *oranje*, but the fruit is a *sinaasappel*—literally, "Chinese apple," on account of China being one of the primary early orange-growing regions. In quite a number of languages, though, the word for orange is based not on the homeland of the fruit, but rather on the traders who brought it to them. Bulgarian, Romanian, Greek, Georgian, Arabic, and even Persian derived their modern words for orange from the name of one of the greatest trading empires in European history: Portugal.

Despite my initial shock, it's actually quite common for a language to have one word that covers both colors. In Vietnamese, *xanh* can refer to blue or to green. If you need to be specific about the shade, then you have to use a compound form: for blue, *xanh da trời* (literally "sky-*xanh*"); for green, *xanh lá cây* (literally "leaf-*xanh*"). Otherwise, *xanh* is perfectly sufficient. These colors can be confusing even when languages have separate words for blue and green—in Japanese the color 青 (*ao*, "blue") is used to describe what is in English practically a Platonic ideal of green: a traffic light.

In some cases, basic color terms in language are *more* specific than what English-speakers may be used to. Hungarian, for instance, has two basic terms for red: *piros*, "red," and *vörös*, "dark red." And Russian has two basic terms for blue: синий (*sinij*) "dark blue," and голубой (*goluboj*), "light blue." If I had a choice, though, between taking a test on a language like Russian or a language like Shona, I'd always choose the more lexically complex option. Color may drive us to absolute distraction when it comes to décor—when I decided to paint my kitchen, it took me more than an hour to choose between Caribbean Coast and Costa Rica Blue. And I'm hardly ever even in my kitchen. In language, however, the truly challenging part isn't learning to name more colors, but learning to name fewer.

ARTICLES AND DETERMINERS

The article is the Old Reliable of English grammar, a part of speech so commonplace that we don't even bother taking it into alphabetic consideration. In many languages, however, articles aren't so mundane. Articles are part of a larger class of modifiers known as determiners, words like "these," "those"; "ours," "yours"; "four," "five"—words that point out exactly which objects or ideas a noun refers to. Adjectives, on the other hand, describe the particular qualities of a noun. A useful if slightly downbeat way to think of the difference between adjectives and determiners is this: if you were mugged on the street, you'd use adjectives when talking to the sketch artist and determiners when picking a suspect out of a lineup.

In a number of languages, including Romanian, Bulgarian, and Albanian, definite articles (the) don't come before the noun, as in English or French, but are instead suffixed to the noun. In Romanian, "a flower" is *o floare*, but "the flower" is *floarea*. The order of Romanian articles and nouns is further complicated by the use of adjectives, which typically follow nouns in Romanian, as in other Romance languages. If you want to emphasize the adjective, however, you can simply place it in front of the noun—in which case you need to attach the article to the adjective instead of the noun. "The good boy," then, has two possible translations, with only minimal variation in meaning: *băiatul bun* or *bunul băiat*.

In many languages, the indefinite article (a/an) is the same as the word for "one," and very often the only way to distinguish between the number and the article is by inference. In Turkish, however, word order helps make things a bit more explicit. When *bir* is used as an article, it immediately precedes the noun: *güzel bir kız* ("a pretty girl"). But when it's used as a number, *bir* precedes the adjective: *bir güzel kız* ("one pretty girl").

I Am Not a Jelly Doughnut

One of the anecdotes most often used to scare language students straight as far as articles go is the story of John F. Kennedy's 1963 speech in West Berlin. As legend has it, when President Kennedy intoned the now-famous words *Ich bin ein Berliner*, his inclusion of the indefinite article *ein* changed the meaning of the sentence from the intended "I am a Berliner" to the much more fun-at-cocktail-parties "I am a jelly doughnut." Although the indefinite article is often left out in German when referring to profession or provenance, the president's meaning was, in this instance, unambiguously clear and perfectly grammatical—if, perhaps, distinctly less entertaining.

In the Celtic language family, articles play a lead role in the grammatical phenomenon most likely to appear in a George Romero film: initial consonantal mutation. In these languages, the first letter of many nouns changes when nouns are paired with articles. Which can be a bit of a shock if you're used to words that only change their endings, as in most other Indo-European languages. And it's even more of a shock when you try looking a word up in a dictionary only to find that you're looking in a completely wrong section. Or so I hear.

In Welsh, whenever you tack on a definite article or the number "one" to a singular feminine noun, you have to change the first letter of the noun according to a particular mutation pattern. The word *pont* (bridge), for instance, becomes *y bont* (the bridge); the word *carreg* (stone) becomes *y garreg* (the stone). Mutation after the definite article in Irish is even more complicated—it occurs in a wide variety of grammatical structures. If you want to use the nominative form of a singular feminine noun with an article, you follow one rule of mutation: *bean* ("woman") becomes *an bhean* ("the woman"). But you have to deal with entirely different rules if you want to use certain adjectives, pronouns, prepositions, and even verbs.

Macedonian is a language that, like Romanian, suffixes its definite articles to the noun or attributive adjective, whichever comes first. The tricky part about Macedonian articles is that the article you use depends on how far away the object is:

женaта (*ženata*)	the woman
женaва (*ženava*)	the woman (here)
женaна (*ženana*)	the woman (there)

It's nothing that can't be said in English with an extra word or two, of course, but it's certainly an elegant construction—and one that I can't help but think could go over awfully well in certain parts of Utah.

Given that two of the most common words in the English language are "the" and "a," it might surprise you to discover that some languages are even more enamored of their articles. In Portuguese, the definite article often shows up before the names of countries, or even of people who aren't Donald Trump. Although Arabic doesn't have an indefinite article, it handily compensates for its relative dearth of determiners by using the definite article before both nouns and adjectives. And French insists on the use of definite articles with abstract nouns that English usually leaves untouched: being, nothingness, nausea.

In other languages, however, articles are used sparingly—or sometimes not at all. Many languages have developed other strategies to indicate whether or not a noun is definite. In Tamil, the accusative case can signal that a neuter noun is definite. In Endo, a Kalenjin language spoken in western Kenya, the nouns themselves shoulder the burden of definiteness: each noun has two separate forms, one definite and one indefinite. And sometimes, definiteness can be communicated through the use of definite or indefinite adjectives, which are found in Serbo-Croatian, Latvian, and Lithuanian, among other languages.

In large part, the definiteness of a Russian noun is up for interpretation. Which, generally, is not such a big deal, unless you've been tasked with translating *War and Peace* or something. In which case articles are probably the least of your worries. But if you really miss the insistent specificity of English, Russian word order can be used to convey the same meaning as an English article. The phrase русские приходят (*russkie prixodjat*), for instance, could mean "Russians are coming" or "the Russians are coming"—which, for many Americans born before 1991, is probably an alarming bit of ambiguity. There's an easy way to ensure the latter meaning, though: just reverse the word order and put the subject after the verb.

Articles and determiners may seem to be essential to an English-speaker, but languages that do without them do just fine. After all, there aren't any articles in Hindi, Mandarin, or Latin, three languages that are rather demonstrably able to say everything they need to say. And, in the case of Latin, often much more than that.

ADVERBS

Of course, the grammar of modifiers isn't always so scintillating. Just take a look at adverbs. Adverbs are typically invariable, which means that grammatically they're a bit like sugar-free candy: stress-free, but, more often than not, disappointingly bland. It doesn't help that, in many languages, adverbs are just dulled-down derivations of adjectives. Think of all the adverbs in English that are simply adjectives with a form of -ly slapped on the end. In most Romance languages, adverbs work in a similar way—you can spot them by picking out the words that end in something close to -*ment*, as in French: *vraiment, follement, profondément* (truly, madly, etc.). You can also make an adverb from an adjective in Modern Greek by changing out an ending or two, as with καλός (*kalos*), "good," and καλά (*kala*), "well." In Old English, many adverbs were derived from adjectives by simply adding an -*e*: *wearm* ("warm"), *wearme* ("warmly").

Word order is about as tasty as grammar gets with respect to adverbs, because you have to worry about not only whether a simple adverb goes before or after the verb, but also how to order adverbial phrases. In English, the order is usually place, manner, time: in the ballroom, with the candlestick, at midnight. German, in contrast, has a rather strict order of time, manner, place: *um Mitternacht, mit dem Kerzenhalter, in dem Ballsaal.*

Another kind of adverb is the disjunctive adverb, a word that can modify an entire clause or an entire sentence. The most infamous English example is "hopefully," that famed bête noir of addled prescriptionist fussbudgets. A few languages—Dutch, Swedish, Danish—have special forms for disjunctive adverbs. In German, for instance, you can take an adjective and add the suffix *-erweise* (from the German word for "manner" or "way") to form a disjunctive adverb, as in *glücklicherweise*, "luckily." Most of the time, however, disjunctive adverbs take the same form as regular old adverbs—they only differ in their placement and the way they are occasionally treated by misguided usage snobs.

And then there are intensifiers (or degree words), which, like the English "really" and "very," can modify other adjectives and adverbs. Intensifiers are another opportunity for languages to indulge their OCD with regard to word order. Most languages also have a preferred order for intensifiers: either before the adjective, as in English, or after the adjective, as in Khmer. Some languages, however, use different orders for different intensifiers. Daniel Everett and Barbara

Kern found that in Pakaásnovos, a language spoken in a few villages in the Brazilian state of Rondônia, 'amon, the word for "a little," precedes the adjective, whereas tamana, the word for "very," follows it.

Many languages have special forms for adjectives that communicate comparative and superlatives, as in the Tibetan yagpo ("good") and yagga ("better") or the Danish god, bedre, bedst. Other languages take another tack, preferring to use adverbs like the English "more" or the Italian più. In Malay, you can make comparatives and superlatives by adding the words lebih and paling: besar, big; lebih besar, bigger; paling besar, biggest. In Bole, a Chadic language spoken in Nigeria, there are no special comparative

---

One Elative Step for Man

In Arabic, the comparative and the superlative are combined into a single inflectional form, the elative. The most common use of the elative in Arabic is found in the *takbīr*, the phrase *Allāhu akbar*, which is commonly translated as "God is great," but means more literally "God is the greatest."

One of the stranger language-related urban legends has Neil Armstrong hearing the *takbīr* (which is included in the Muslim call to prayer) when he first walked on the moon, an experience that resulted in his conversion to Islam. The story was so pervasive that the U.S. State Department issued

a memo denying the story in the hopes that Armstrong might stop receiving, as the memo tersely put it, "communications from individuals and religious organizations, and a feeler from at least one government, about his possible participation in religious activities."

or superlative forms, with or without adverbs—to say "I'm taller than you," you would instead have to use a construct that literally means "My height surpasses that of you."

In my experience, intensifiers in English are, like the embattled and misunderstood disjunctive adverbs, a fairly maligned group of words. But the problem with intensifiers isn't how you use them, but rather what you choose to use. In America in particular, the use of certain colloquial intensifiers is often seized upon as a sort of linguistic gateway to the dark parts of the soul. If, for instance, you say "wicked"—as in "wicked cool" or the venerable "wicked pissah"—there are those who might assume that you root for the Red Sox—and may be, at that very moment, drunk. And if you use the word "totally," well, you must either be between the ages of eight and eighteen or unforgivably empty-headed.

I can't say whether intensifiers are objects of particular derision because they tend to be more geographically specific, because there is a sort of deep cultural distrust of linguistic embellishment, or because I'm just sensitive about the fact that I say "totally" all the time. And am decidedly not between the ages of eight and eighteen. Modern modifiers may no longer cause such widespread controversy as the nineteenth-century adjective, but in some cases they're still struggling for widespread acceptance. I'm reminded of a quote from Strunk and White's *The*

Elements of Style, that venerable guide to English style and usage. In it, White stated, "Write with nouns and verbs, not with adjectives and adverbs. The adjective hasn't been built that can pull a weak or inaccurate noun out of a tight place." When I first read Strunk and White, I happened to be particularly smitten with style guides, and I remember doing my very best to chop out all of the offending adjectives from my school papers. Years later, however, after taking a turn through the world's adjectives and adverbs and relishing their capabilities and curiosities, the above suggestion elicits an entirely different response: that's bloody stupid.

SPEECH

Each time a polling group or news team decides to conduct a survey on fear, the usual suspects are to blame for keeping people in a state of perpetual terror: death, hell, debt, snakes, etc. But there's another phobia that, surprisingly, shows up again and again: public speaking. Even though the world is full of appalling, spine-chilling atrocities, for many of us, talking to a group of people—people who are not, presumably, armed with weapons or a stack of credit reports—manages to rank in our collective top ten no-can-dos.

I can't say that I entirely disagree. Given the choice between public speech or death, sure, I'd choose public speech. But given the choice between public speech and snakes, I'd probably take snakes. Because snakes won't remember if I make a fool of myself.

Language requires more than mere mastery of noun declensions and verb conjugations. Replicating the sounds of language and abiding by its social conventions demand a complex and subtle understanding not only of pronunciation, but also of propriety and intention. Studying a language in a book is easy; speaking a language, however, is anything but.

Which is probably why I've saved this section for last.

BASIC PRONUNCIATION

The sounds of language often elude simple, precise description—if you don't have a background in phonetics, that is. Many language books get around the problem of pronunciation by including long lists of "as in" tips, things like "pronounced 'd' as in 'dog'" or "'k' as in 'key.'" But when languages have sound systems that are radically different than English, the "as-in" formula becomes less and less useful. First you start seeing lots of words like "similar to" or "almost like" next to the English equivalents. Then you might start seeing references to particular dialects: I have one book that recommends approaching the Malay "aa" sound as if I were speaking Cockney English; I have another that suggests keeping in mind the "southern British English" pronunciation of "put" when tackling similar sounds in Cantonese. Which I'm sure is tremendously helpful if you can replicate a Cockney accent or have the slightest clue what a southern British English dialect sounds like. I, unfortunately, cannot and do not. Eventually, many language books give up on English altogether and either use another language as an example ("'ch' as in the German *Buch*") or attempt to evoke the sound by other means. One of my Arabic phrasebooks includes a guide to pronunciation that describes the Arabic letter *ḥā'* as having "no English equivalent; pronounced by sharply exhaling air from the throat as if blowing onto eyeglasses."

. . .

While "sounds like" illustrations certainly get the general idea across, I often find that it's easier to cut to the chase and consult the phonetic terminology,

Uvular Trill

Possible Entries in My Series of Linguistic Erotica

Alveolar Ejective

Retroflex Flap

Uvular Trill

Bilabial Fricative

Diphthong

the terms that linguists use to describe the position of the tongue, teeth, and lips required for sounds and the type of air used to create those sounds. (Phonetic terminology is also tremendously appealing to my particularly juvenile sense of humor: if I were ever to write a bodice-ripping linguist romance, I would skip the obvious pun and instead rely solely on phonetic terms.)

Take the French "r," a sound that has caused generations of students significant pain and confusion. When you try to describe the French "r" in general terms, you often get something like "pronounced in the back of throat," or "kind of swallowed." The *Lonely Planet Phrasebook* for French makes this charming suggestion: "It's quite similar to the noise made by some people before spitting." If you're willing to put up with some linguistic terminology, though, things make a lot more sense: the sound is classified as a "uvular trill" or "uvular fricative," which means that the back of the tongue taps against the uvula—something that is significantly easier to do than howking up a loogie every time you want to say *rien*.

Another particularly tricky consonant sound for many native speakers of European languages is the retroflex consonant. Retroflex sounds require the tip of the tongue to turn back slightly. Try saying "dog" as you normally would, and then say it again with your tongue turned up and touching the roof of your mouth a little farther back than you're used

BITING THE WAX TADPOLE

to—it should sound a little bit like you're sneaking an "l" sound in there. Retroflex consonants are very common in Indo-Aryan and Dravidian languages like Hindi, Tamil, and Sanskrit. The initial "r" used in the roman transliteration of Mandarin is also a retroflex sound—a retroflex fricative, to be exact—which can sound like a combination of an r, an l, and a j. This is, for English-speakers, one of the hardest sounds in Mandarin to reproduce—which is rather unfortunate, really, given that it occurs in really common words like 人 (*rén*; person) and 日 (*rì*; sun).

Yet another fun sound is the glottal stop, which is marked in some languages with an apostrophe, and others with a modified question mark (ʔ). A glottal stop is technically a "glottal plosive," which means that the air flow is stopped up by contracting your glottis (what you do when you hold your breath) and then expelling a bit of air. English-speakers sometimes slip glottal stops between words that end and begin with vowels—carefully enunciate "Eerie, Indiana" and you'll hear (and feel) what I mean. There are few words in English, however, that incorporate glottal stops, so it can take a bit of getting used to when a language uses them more frequently, as in the Tahitian *pua'a* (pig) or the Hawai'ian *Hawai'i*. In Navajo, the single most common consonantal sound is the glottal stop, and any word with an initial vowel actually begins with one. So a word like *atł'aa'* (buttocks) requires a total of three glottal stops—not an easy feat.

In most languages, the force used to create a sound comes from the lungs (these sounds are known as "pulmonic"). But there are non-pulmonic sounds in language, too—including one of the most enduringly quixotic of all sounds in language, the click. Click consonants either use the air that's already in the mouth to create a sound or they suck air in from the outside. Even though clicks aren't part of the standard phonological inventory of English, they aren't entirely absent from English speech (particularly if you happen to work with animals or engage in disgusting displays of public affection with your significant other). But, as with the glottal stop, these sounds aren't incorporated into words in English, which is one reason why languages that use clicks sound so very different. I suspect that another reason clicks are so exoticized has to do with their transliteration. One particular click is marked by a symbol that looks very much like an exclamation mark, which has resulted in legions of bad jokes about the excited appearance of languages like !Kung. (Which, by the way, has 48 distinct click consonants—and that's in addition to 47 non-click consonants.)

• • •

For the most part, click consonants are concentrated in a number of sub-Saharan African languages, including the Khoisan languages and a number of

Bantu languages. The only non-African language known to employ clicks as regular speech sounds is Damin, a secret ritual language used by speakers of Lardil in Australia. Damin is particularly noteworthy because it has two types of really unusual sounds. One is a variation on the clicks described above, except instead of an ingressive sound (think about making a kissing noise—you're actually sucking in air), Damin also uses an egressive click, which means that you have to push the air out without using any air from your lungs.

Another atypical sound in Damin is the pulmonic ingressive, which requires a full-on inhalation instead of an exhalation. Although ingressive sounds are used

A Few Relatively Simple
Click Consonants

NAME	SYMBOL	ROUGH APPROXIMATION
bilabial	☉	an ostentatious smooching sound
dental	ǀ	a sarcastically disappointed "tsk"
alveolar	ǃ	an imitation of a tocking (not ticking) clock
lateral	ǁ	that annoying noise people use to urge on horses

in very few languages, they sometimes show up in surprising places. In some Scandinavian languages, including Norwegian, Swedish, and Danish, the word *ja* (yes) is occasionally said on an inhalation— in practice, it sounds a lot like a gasp, or a sharply indrawn breath. When I first tried to make the sound, though, I thought that my vocal cords were also supposed to vibrate—and thank god I only tried to do that in the privacy of my own home, because it made me sound like Humphrey Bogart crossed with Harvey Fierstein.

Not all languages are so complicated, however. If an impenetrable phonetic inventory scares you off, you might want to consider a Polynesian language instead. Tahitian, Samoan, Tongan, and Maori, among others, typically use very few consonants. (Hawai'ian, for instance has only eight: p, k, h, m, n, l, w, and a glottal stop.) Because of this, consonants are never clustered as in the word "sing"—or "word," for that matter—so there are an extremely limited number of possible sound combinations. There are only 162 possible syllables in Hawai'ian; Thai, in stark contrast, has more than twenty thousand.

PROSODY

Stress, tone, intonation, and rhythm also play a part in making language the incredibly rich and communicative medium it is. These features of speech, collectively known as prosody, can prove to be even more difficult than plain old phonetics. English makes a clear distinction between speech and song, but in many languages the line isn't so simple, and anyone who has ever stumbled through a choral rehearsal may lament the various ways that languages use volume and pitch. (Admission: I once had a choral master tell me my singing was so bad as to be "anatomically impossible.")

One of the simplest prosodic features of language for English-speakers is stress. A language is said to have a "stress accent" if its speakers emphasize certain syllables of certain words by raising the volume of their voices. Occasionally, a stress accent can be used to differentiate between two words that would otherwise sound the same, as in the English words "refill" or "defect." Much to my chagrin, however, stress isn't formally marked in English, so it's easy to read a word and then try to work it into a conversation with a slightly unusual pronunciation. In fact, for most of my life, I thought "chagrin" was pronounced "CHAH-grin." And I'm still kind of unclear about the proper stress of "inclement."

Other languages have more concrete rules for where the stress falls. In Latin, the pattern of the stress accent is extremely regular. If you have a two-syllable word, the stress goes on the first syllable: *veni, vidi, vici*. With words of three syllables or more, the stress either falls on the second-to-last or third-to-last syllable, depending on whether or not the penultimate syllable is long. Some languages make it even easier: the stress accent in Finnish is always on the first syllable. In Macedonian, the stress falls on the antepenult (the third syllable before the end). The Sámi languages have a rhythmic stress pattern in which odd syllables are stressed and even syllables are unstressed—which for some might call to mind "The Song of Hiawatha," but rather reminds me of *One Fish, Two Fish, Red Fish, Blue Fish*.

Although Modern Greek has a stress accent similar to that of English, Ancient Greek had a slightly different system. The accent in Ancient Greek is known as a "pitch accent," which means that stressed syllables don't vary in volume, but rather in pitch. The Ancient Greek pitch accent was marked with diacritics beginning in about the ninth century A.D., so you can pretty much crack open any Ancient Greek text today and see concrete evidence of the old pitch-accent system. If you see an acute accent in an Ancient Greek text—Ζεύς (Zeus) or Σωκράτης (Socrates)—it means that the accented syllable was originally spoken on a slightly higher pitch than the rest. With a grave accent, the opposite is true—the accented syllable is pitched slightly lower than the rest. The pitch of a syllable with a circumflex accent, on the other hand, raises and lowers: Σοφοκλῆς (Sophocles) or Περικλῆς (Pericles).

• • •

Pitch accent is by no means a phenomenon confined to drunken recitations of the Odyssey at Classics department keg parties. The characters for "salmon" and "sake" (the beverage, that is) are the same in Japanese: さけ (*sake*). In the standard Tokyo dialect, if the first syllable is higher than the second, the word means "salmon." If the second syllable is higher than the first, though, it means "sake." Pretend you're asking a question: "sake?" That's the pronunciation for the booze. Then pretend you're answering the question: "sake." That's the pronunciation for the fish. As in English, though, accent is unmarked in written Japanese and has to be learned either by rote or by regular humiliation.

And pitch accent doesn't just distinguish between different words. Some languages use pitch accent for grammatical purposes as well. In Somali, a shift in the pitch accent can indicate a change in gender, as in *ínan* (boy) and *inán* (girl). It can also indicate a change in number: *árday* (student), *ardáy* (students). Pitch accent is also the feature that gives so many Scandinavian languages their distinctive singsong quality. Quite a few two-syllable words in Swedish are distinguished solely by their different pitch accents: *anden*, for instance, can mean either "duck" or "spirit," depending on where you place the accent.

Pitch accent is often conflated with another prosodic feature: tone. The linguistic use of the word "tone" is different from the way the word is more commonly used in everyday speech, as in "Don't use that tone with me, young lady." When tone is applied to an entire sentence—when asking a question in English—it's called "intonation." A tonal language, however, is a language that assigns a different pitch or combination of pitches to every syllable in a word—which is in turn different from a language with a pitch accent, which only assigns a pitch to *one* syllable within a word.

The types of tone that are used in the world's languages vary wildly. Mandarin has five tones. The first tone is the high hold-steady tone that I'm apparently incapable of properly replicating—to try it yourself, think about sticking your tongue out at the doctor's office and saying "Aaaah." The second tone is a rising tone similar to the sound made in English at the end of a question. The third tone is trickier: it's a low tone that falls and then rises. The closest approximation I can think of is the skeptical sound you might make when encouraging someone to continue with some clearly fallacious reasoning: "Okaaaay." The fourth tone is a sharp falling tone, what you'd use when you let loose a curse word. And the last tone is known as the "netural" tone. Its pronunciation isn't fixed—it depends on the tone that comes before it.

The Language of Furniture That Never Looks as Good Once You Get It Home

Thanks to the corporate monster that is IKEA, thousands of Americans probably know more Swedish words than words they remember from high-school Spanish. As part of their strategy for low-cost world domination, IKEA doesn't bother with item names that require translation, turning instead to Swedish for names that surely seem far more exotic and luxurious to English-speakers than the products themselves deserve. And, much like the diabolical layout of IKEA stores, there's often a method to the product-naming madness: bookshelves, for instance, are often named after occupations (*bonde*, farmer; *expedit*, salesman). Curtain accessories, bizarrely, are sometimes tagged with mathematical terms—*täljare*, the name for a style of curtain rod, also means "numerator." And when the bed-linen naming committee isn't half-assing things with names like *sova* (sleep) and *tupplur* (nap), they'll pick names of flowers and plants—although why anyone would want a quilt cover called *kaktus*, I don't know.

Talking Drums

Tonal languages present considerable challenges to the novice language-learner, but they offer native speakers serious communicative advantages. Many African cultures use a system of drumming that replicates the tones of language to relay messages across long distances.

The drummers transmit messages of astounding complexity—a complexity that's intensified by the necessity of avoiding ambiguity. In Bukala, a dialect of the Bantu language Mongo-Nkundu, the words *songe* (moon) and *kaka* (fowl) both consist of two high tones. But as John F. Carrington,

a missionary in the then-Belgian Congo, discovered, a drummer can distinguish between the two with a bit of elaboration: "moon" becomes a tonal rendition of "the moon looks down at the earth," and "fowl" is stretched out to "the fowl, the little one that says 'kiokio.'"

BITING THE WAX TADPOLE

But tones don't only vary across languages; they can vary within languages, too. And many Chinese dialects have quite different tonal patterns: the tonal system of Shanghainese is so different from standard Mandarin that it might even be classified as a pitch-accent language. At the other end of the spectrum is Cantonese, which has anywhere between six and nine tones, depending on whom you ask.

Tonal languages aren't restricted to East and Southeast Asia, although they're certainly very prevalent in that area—in addition to Chinese, Thai, Lao, and Vietnamese are also tonal. But many sub-Saharan African languages also make extensive use of tone. Mòoré, one of the major languages of Burkina Faso, has three tones: high, low, and a falling-rising tone; Hausa has two: high and low. Most Bantu languages are tonal, too—in this, Swahili, arguably the best-known Bantu language and otherwise representative of many features shared by the language family, is a notable exception.

As with pitch accent, there are two uses of tone: lexical tone, which changes the meaning of the word, as in Mandarin and Zulu, and grammatical tone, in which the tone of a word can alter its grammatical function. In Ngiti, a Nilo-Saharan language spoken in the Democratic Republic of the Congo, tonal variation can signal changes in verb tense and aspect: *ma màkpěnà* means "I whistled," but *ma makpéna* means "I will whistle." The Kenyan language of Rendille, on the other hand, can use tone to distinguish grammatical case. If you want to use *inam* (boy) as the object of a verb, you have to change the tone of the first syllable to a high tone: *ínam*. (Another vexing aspect of tone is that the diacritical marks used to indicate tone also vary from language to language. So although in transliterated Mandarin an acute accent indicates a rising tone, in Ngiti and Rendille it signifies a high level tone.)

In many languages, tones undergo complicated changes when in conjunction with other tones—a process known as tone sandhi (from the Sanskrit word for "putting together"). In Mandarin, whenever two third tones are butted up against each other, the first changes to a rising tone. So the standard greeting 你好 (*nǐ hǎo*) is actually pronounced *ní hǎo*. When multiple high tones occur successively in Akan, a language spoken primarily in Ghana, each tone is slightly lower than the one that came before. Cháozhōu, a Chinese dialect spoken in Guangdong, has ten tones, and every single one of them changes when in combination.

Sometimes, tone turns out to be much more complicated than mere variation in pitch. You may stumble across a language guide that claims that Burmese has four tones. But each "tone" actually combines pitch with intensity, duration, and phonation (which means, at its simplest, the way that the vocal cords vibrate to create a given sound). The

The Lion-Eating Poet in the Stone Den

In the early twentieth century, the Chinese linguist Yuen Ren Chao wrote a ninety-two character poem in Classical Chinese called "The Lion-Eating Poet in the Stone Den." In its written form, the poem is perfectly understandable: the first line reads "In a stone den was a poet Shi who loved to eat lions and decided to eat ten." But when the poem is read with modern Chinese pronunciations, it's a little less clear. The first line reads like this: *Shíshì shīshì Shī Shì, shì shí shī, shì shí shí shī.* And it just keeps going—ninety-two repetitions of a single syllable. Not even the most tonally adept among us would have a damn clue what that's supposed to mean.

Burmese system is so different from the tonal system of a language like Mandarin that it is instead said to have separate "registers." The low register combines a low and sometimes slightly rising pitch with medium duration and regular old phonation. Then things get a little difficult. The high register takes a high pitch and long length and adds to it a "breathy" voice— breathy sounds are still voiced, which means that you can still feel your throat vibrate if you put your hand against it, so it's not exactly a whisper, but the vocal cords are held slightly farther apart to give the sound a certain old-Hollywood sexpot flavor. And then there's the "creaky" register, which requires the vocal cords to vibrate much more slowly than usual— make like that creepy lady in *The Grudge*, and you'll probably be able to approximate the sound. The final register in Burmese requires the addition of a glottal stop to the end of a syllable and is known as the "checked" or, more colorfully, "killed" register.

Suffice it to say, I'm not exactly expecting to be able to pick up Burmese anytime soon.

RESPECT

It may come as a great shock to those who are under the impression that Parisians hold the worldwide monopoly on rude behavior, but the language that introduced me to the grammatical structure of politeness and respect was French. In my fourth year of French class, my teacher decided that we had finally progressed to the point where we could leave behind our tourist-trap textbook dialogues and dig into an actual book. We weren't proficient enough to tackle anything too heady (such is the snail's pace of middle-school language classes—three full years and we still couldn't read a book), so our introduction to French literature came in the guise of a slim novel called *Suivez la piste*—"Follow the Trail!" In keeping with our limited language skills, it had all the literary sophistication of a middle-grade edition of *The Da Vinci Code*. Camus, it was not.

The book featured two main characters, Dacier and Catherine, destined from page one to fall in love. But the book was written with impressionable young students in mind, so the actual details of their consummation were not divulged. Instead, there was a mundane morning-after scene in which neither character alluded to recent developments in any overt manner. Except for one thing: in a sharp about-face, they suddenly began to use familiar verb forms with each other. Which made matters as clear to a classroom of hormonally astute fifteen-year-olds as if they had stumbled down to breakfast in flagrante. At that moment, *tutoyer* took on a whole new meaning for me.

In French and in many other languages, respect and formality can be conveyed through specialized vocabularies and with specific grammatical forms. In French, you use the second-person plural pronoun (*vous*) and attendant verb form when addressing a stranger or superior or someone you want to impress; when talking to friends, children, animals, or someone you just don't like, then you use the second-person singular pronoun (*tu*).

The use of various pronouns for different formal or informal situations is so prevalent that it gets its own jargon: the "T-V distinction," after the Latin second-person pronouns *tū* and *vōs*. In Serbo-Croatian, the singular *ti* is used with friends and family, whereas the plural *vi* is used (and capitalized) in formal situations; Scottish Gaelic uses the singular *thu* informally and the plural *sibh* formally.

English also used to have a more explicit distinction between formal and informal pronouns. Although "thou" and "thee" may sound antiquated and, therefore, formal to modern ears, at one point they were, respectively, the informal singular nominative and accusative pronouns. "You" and "ye," meanwhile, served as their formal (and plural) counterparts. This is not, as it turns out, a feature of Old English, but rather something that was picked up along the way, likely from French.

"Thou" and "thee" were already falling out of use by the eighteenth century, but an interesting twist of fate has resulted in their preservation in a few isolated pockets. The linguistic counterpart to the Quaker belief in plain dress was plain speech, in which everyone, regardless of social standing, was addressed with familiar pronouns to emphasize the fundamental Quaker belief in egalitarianism. At the time, though, the familiar forms were "thou" and "thee." As a result, many Quaker communities in the United States were still using "thou" and "thee" as personal pronouns through the mid-twentieth century.

Second-person pronouns don't bear full responsibility for formality and informality, though. Italian now uses the third-person feminine singular as the formal pronoun, regardless of the gender of the addressee in question. Telugu, a language spoken primarily in the Indian state of Andhra Pradesh on the Bay of Bengal, has not only separate polite forms for second-person pronouns, but also three levels of formality for its third-person pronouns: familiar, respectful, and honorific. And English still occasionally uses a first-person plural to connote an element of superiority, as in the "royal we." Which, I've noticed lately, has been heavily co-opted by the blogosphere in the form of the (deeply ironic) "editorial we."

In some languages, it's possible to indicate a level of respect even in the absence of pronouns and verbs. Kannada, another Indian language and the official language of Karnataka, slaps on a double plural to indicate respect: you can take the plural endings -*aru* and -*galu* and add them on to a word as a sort of reverent plural, as in *dēvarugaḷu,* "gods." Meanwhile, Malayalam, an Indian language not to be confused with Malay, has a dedicated honorific plural suffix: *amma,* "mother," becomes *ammamār,* "mothers."

But none of these languages come close to the sociolinguistic intricacy of Balinese and Javanese. Javanese has two levels of respect (*ngoko* for informal usage and *kråmå* for polite usage), and Balinese has a full three (*basa ketah,* for friends and family; *basa madia,* for slightly more formal uses; and *basa singgih,* for unmistakably formal situations). Although the grammar for each level of respect is the same in each language, the vocabulary is drastically different. Take a word like "eat," for instance. In Balinese, there are three ways to say "eat," depending on the necessary level of formality: *naar, neda,* and *ngadjengang.* If you want to be fluent in Balinese, then, you pretty much have to learn to use three separate vocabularies. And also, of course, to be loudly, painfully aware of your social standing at all times. I imagine it's a lot like high school.

A few languages also feature something called "avoidance speech." It's similar to the formal levels of Javanese and Balinese in that avoidance speech typically uses the same grammar as the standard language, differing only in the lexicon. Avoidance speech can be used when in the presence of members of the opposite sex or during initiation rituals. The Batak languages in Indonesia, for example, have separate words and forms for use at deathbeds and burials.

In Dyirbal, the Australian language of women, fire, and dangerous things, the everyday language is called Guwal. But until relatively recently (the linguist R. M. W. Dixon noted that the practice had fallen out of use around 1930), whenever Dyirbal speakers were in the presence of certain relatives they would have to switch to Dyalnguy, the avoidance language. What's particularly interesting about Dyalnguy is that its vocabulary is more limited than that of the everyday language. As a result, avoidance terms tend to be generic, whereas everyday terms are quite specific. So although Guwal has separate words for "shake," "wave," and "smash" (*baygun*, *dyindan*, and *banyin*, respectively), Dyalnguy has just one term for all three: *bubaman*.

Perhaps the most revealing insight to come from avoidance languages, however, is that one relative in particular seems to require the lion's share of avoidance speech, which is why there's an alternate name for the phenomenon: mother-in-law language.

DISRESPECT

On the flip side of all of this proper, well-meaning speech is, of course, profanity. Or, as I often think of it, humankind's great cultural legacy. If ever there were evidence of humanity's creative spirit, it's to be found in the stunning variety of curse words that people have come up with over the centuries. Just to give you a small idea of the breadth of profanity in the world, I have a book of Russian obscenities that includes dozens of different words for flatulence alone.

Profanity comes in four basic subject areas—sex, bodily functions, religion, and family—and the subject area of greatest potential offense tends to vary from culture to culture. Blasphemy in many parts of the United States is, for example, becoming less and less unseemly. This is far from true in other countries, however. Italian, unsurprisingly, is full of religious curses and oaths—an easy way to create your own Italian profanity is to take the name of a farm animal (pig is a popular choice) and combine it with a religious figure: *porca Eva, porco Dio, porca Madonna.*

One of the most well-known Finnish curse words is *perkele*, a word that originally referred to a pagan thunder-god but soon came to be equated with the devil. In Quebec, many curse words have a strong connection to Catholicism, but they're often such everyday words that the profanity is almost refreshing. (This particular set of curse words is known in Quebec as *les sacres*—from the verb *sacrer*, "to consecrate.") The single most famous Quebecois swear word is *tabarnac*, a shortened form of *tabernacle.* Other popular choices include *câlice* (chalice) and *baptême* (baptism). My particular favorites, though, are the toned-down swear words designed for more general usage. *Sacrament*, for instance, can be replaced with *sac à papier*—literally, "paper bag."

Quebec French isn't the only language to have a wide range of euphemisms so that we don't have to sacrifice our need to talk about impolite subject matter even when we're in polite company. In Chinese, 豆腐 (*dòufǔ*; tofu) can be a polite word for "breasts." In Spanish, *huevos* (eggs) can also be used to mean "testicles." And I won't even get into the universally fraught linguistic position of roosters and cats. A knowledge of profanity may be useful, but a familiarity with euphemism is downright necessary, if only because the world is full of people who'd like nothing more than to laugh at your

The Idiot

Of all the insults in the world, rarely have I found one so charming as 馬鹿 (*baka*), a Japanese word for "idiot." As with many bits of profanity, the story behind its origin is as entertaining as it is unlikely: as legend has it, a hopeless Chinese king once mistakenly identified a deer (鹿; *ka*) as a horse (馬; *ba*), simultaneously earning the phrase *baka* the timeless honor of referring to someone who can't tell two very different animals apart and coming up with one of the most succinct definitions of "idiot" I've ever heard.

unintentional double entendres. I know because I'm one of them—I still twitter every time I think about a particular vegetarian restaurant in New York. It's called Gobo, after the Japanese 牛蒡 (*gobō*), which means "burdock root." And is also slang for "penis."

Any buttoned-down language teacher who feels that profanity has no place in the classroom need look only so far as Latin to find a compelling counterargument. Latin has a truly delightful tradition of profanity, something I admit to having been rather shocked by in high school, when all of the otherwise-staid Classics students were hard at work translating the profoundly dirty poetry of Catullus. Much to my lingering regret, I never studied Latin in high school, and the Ancient Greek texts I translated tended to relate to respectable subjects like justice and ethics and whether or not Socrates was pissed off about his crappy death sentence. (I will say, however, that Socrates did have one great oath: "By the dog of Egypt!") Meanwhile, everyone over in the Latin classrooms got to discuss erotic poetry and eat doughnuts.

With this in mind, I wrote to three friends who took Latin in high school to ask if they remembered any of the language's seedier bits. Almost immediately, all three were able to respond not only with anecdotes, but with grammar, vocabulary, and even lines of poetry. One of my favorites is *salaputium*, a word with a literal meaning of "little man" but a more inclusive sense of "a man with disproportionately small genitals." I can't help but think that the Classicists may have stumbled on a supremely effective pedagogical tactic: dirty up your language classes, and kids will pay more attention.

Profanity can be a tough thing to get a handle on, because in languages that are not, like Latin, embalmed and unchanging, the use of profanity tends to vary widely from dialect to dialect and region to region. Consider the vast differences between American, British, and Australian profanity. An American wouldn't think twice about using the word "fanny" to indicate a child's rear end, but if you were to say the same thing in Britain you might get thrown in jail.

It doesn't help that so many guides to language-learning tend to be a bit persnickety about the whole thing. Even when you do find a guide to slang or profanity (which will often be unnecessarily plastered with warnings about potentially offensive content in a wholly futile attempt to prove their street cred), chances are that many of the words will either be out of date or only useful in very specific circumstances. Of all the aspects of language, slang is surely the hardest to get down in book form—it changes so fast. Honestly, the best way to go about picking up dirty words is to go to the country of your choice and hang out with teenagers, the foul-mouthed linguistic ambassadors of the world.

But any effort you have to go to is worth it. Because if you do manage to pick up some profanity, it'll stay with you for life. I have no doubt that the last of my French to go will be *va te faire foutre*.

Luckily, I can't think of a phrase—in any language—that I'd ever need more.

CONCLUSION

In college, my Mandarin curriculum focused heavily on politics, which was immensely frustrating for a number of reasons. For one thing, after a year of intensive study I knew how to say "one-child policy," but I had never learned the word for "shoes." And trust me, Shanghai shopkeepers were already laughing hard enough at my Yeti-sized feet without my trying to buy "things my feet like." Another problem related to our reading material: each week I was stuck translating an article about one political development or another. And even though I'd learned to recognize Chinese names, I had a hell of a time with Western names. Each time I saw the characters 克林顿, I'd start looking them up one by one. And then I'd stare grimly at my translation and wonder just what the hell "repress forest pause" was supposed to mean. More often than not it wasn't until some kindly professor would read the characters out loud for me—*kèlíndùn*—and I'd

---

Presidential Address

GEORGE WASHINGTON

乔治 · 华盛顿

qiáozhì huáshèngdùn

disguise govern, magnificent abundant pause

THOMAS JEFFERSON

托玛斯 · 杰弗逊

tūomǎsī jiéfùxùn

entrust agate cut, hero not modest

JOHN (F.) KENNEDY

约翰 · 肯尼迪

yuēhàn kěnnédí

treaty feather, willing-to nun advance

JIMMY CARTER

吉米 · 卡特

jǐmǐ kǎtè

lucky rice, card bull

BILL CLINTON

比尔 · 克林顿

bǐ'ěr kèlíndùn

compare lattice, repress forest pause

GEORGE WALKER BUSH

乔治 · 沃克 · 布什

qiáozhì wòkè bùshí

disguise govern, irrigate repress, announce squad

realize that once again, I had completely forgotten the Chinese for "Clinton."

Translating proper names into foreign languages is notoriously challenging, and it's even more daunting in a language like Chinese, which uses characters instead of a phonetic script. As each character has a meaning as well as a sound associated with it, anything you translate phonetically is also going to have its own separate meaning.

So when Coca-Cola was introduced in China in 1928, the task of translating the product name into Chinese was far from trivial. Eventually, the company offered a cash reward for anyone who could come up with an appropriate translation. The winner was 可口可乐 (kěkǒu kělè), a phrase loosely translated as "delicious happiness." Needless to say, the brand name worked—not only is Coca-Cola hugely popular in China, but the word 可乐 (kělè) has come to be used as the standard Mandarin word for any kind of soft drink.

But there was a bit of lag time between the product launch and its Chinese christening, which meant that Chinese shopkeepers had to come up with their own way to advertise the new beverage in the meantime. Many used characters that sounded even closer to the original: 可口蝌蜡 (kěkǒu kēlà). Which is all well and good from a phonetic standpoint—until you translate the meaning. For a while, you could travel to Shanghai and order yourself up a bottle of "bite the wax tadpole." I know you're getting thirsty just thinking about it.

Despite the many reports to the contrary, Coca-Cola didn't have anything to do with the less-than-tasty translation. It's my guess that shopkeepers figured, given the absurdity of the phrase, that no fluent Chinese-speaker would mistake it for anything other than a transliteration—just as no fluent Chinese-speaker would confuse President Clinton with a repressed forest pause.

Ironically, however, the tadpole story has legs. It's gone from amusing anecdote to a business fable of Aesopian proportions. Today it's used all over as a prime example of how not to translate your product name into another language (ignoring, of course, the rather important fact that Coca-Cola handled things quite competently on their end). I can certainly understand the dangers of mistranslation—from a business perspective. After all, no one wants to spend millions of dollars on a product launch only to have it laughed out of stores. In business, you get it right or go home.

But had I gone home the first time I flubbed a phrase in China, I would have lost something far more important than market share. Because I wouldn't have had the chance to watch the sun rise from the summit of Huangshan—or face down an angry monkey on the slopes of Jiuhuashan. I would have missed out on lovely, leisurely nights

And Now a Poorly Chosen Word From Our Sponsors

The single most widely cited example of a foreign-marketing foul-up comes at the expense of Chevrolet, which introduced the Chevy Nova in Mexico in 1972. As the story goes, sales of the new model were anemic due to the fact that Nova sounds a great deal like the Spanish *no va,* or "doesn't go." It would be a cute story—if it were true. In reality, "Nova" was no more mistaken for *no va* than "noble" is for "no bull," and sales were just fine. That's not to say that General Motors has a perfect record when it comes to translation. In 2003, GM was forced to rename the Buick La Crosse in Canada when it was discovered that the name also happened to be Quebecois slang—for masturbation.

picking up peanuts with chopsticks and watching *A Chinese Ghost Story 2.* I would never have been chased through a village in Hubei by a child who was shouting "Monster, monster!"

Instead, I would have headed immediately to the airport as soon as I realized I'd told a cab driver to take me to Shanghai University (*shànghǎi dàxué*), which was a good half-hour away from my intended destination, a hotel near Shanghai Mansions (*shànghǎi dàshà*). A cab driver who had, by the way, picked me up *from* said airport.

•   •   •

When I tell people about my affection for foreign languages, one of three things inevitably happens:

1. I discover that I'm in equally linguistically obsessed company, and we enter into an unrepentantly geeked-out discussion of the vagaries of grammatical minutiae.

2. My companions suddenly realize they have to refill their drinks/go to the bathroom/attend to an unexpected medical emergency.

3. I hear the words "You know, I'm just not a language person."

The third scenario is slightly less frequent than the second, but even so, I can't count the number of times I've heard someone claim to be simply unable to dig into language. Whether it's memorization-related misgivings, anxiety about grammatical jargon, or post-high-school-Spanish stress disorder, there's always something holding them back, something that makes them believe they're unequipped to learn another language.

But the truth is this: if you speak a language, you're cut out for language. What varies from person to person is the ability to master a new tongue, not the ability to enjoy it. You don't have to have been a straight-A student to be able to appreciate all the intricacies, oddities, and viewpoints the world's languages have to offer. After all, if we based our future interests on our high school behavior, right now I'd be pursuing a career in hiding in corners and listening to the Smiths.

For me, language isn't just an opportunity to flex my mental muscles. Whether I'm traveling abroad or sitting at home, language is nothing less than a great adventure. It's full of culture, history, humor. And, yes, sometimes even humiliation. Language is, at its heart, about humanity—and there's nothing more human than being humbled. But even though I may misconstrue verbs or mispronounce words, the only real mistake I can make is to let the things I might get wrong keep me from finding out what's right.

Only a lucky few of us will ever have the opportunity to hop from city to city and country to country, to see all we want to see of what the world has to show. But that doesn't mean we have to miss

Under-publicized Reasons for Learning a New Language

Rewarding conversations with long-distance tech support

Japanese game shows

Q-without-U Scrabble words

Telenovelas

Finally making sense of *The Waste Land*

Big Brother: Bulgaria

Being able to ensure that your Chinese tattoo does not, in fact, say "crazy diarrhea" out on all the fun. There are nearly seven thousand known living languages in the world, and each one is an odyssey of its own. Don't let fear keep you from finding out firsthand. Pick up a grammar guide, listen to a language tape, turn on a foreign film. Let go of your doubts, uncertainties, and insecurities and start exploring—there are worlds out there just waiting to be discovered.

And here's a head start: *bon voyage.*

ACKNOWLEDGMENTS

This book owes its existence to the fearless, tireless efforts of Becky Kraemer and everyone else at Melville House. If only every publishing house were privileged enough to have access to such spirit, skill, and wit. I am more grateful for their support than I can say.

I am also profoundly indebted to Cindy Price and Jeff Klein, the first to wonder if my musings might merit publication.

Many thanks to those who read the book in its early stages and provided indispensable advice and encouragement, linguistic and otherwise: Alison Cherry, John Herndon, Ellen Guimbarda, Leigh Maltese, and Annie Ronan. Kate Naunheim deserves special mention for having an impressively thorough and profane grasp of Latin vocabulary. Any remaining errors in grammar (or judgment) are entirely my own.

None of this would have been possible without the incredible kindness and incomparable patience of Kate Garrick, whose wisdom and friendship I would never want to do without. And I cannot begin to enumerate the contributions of Dylan Kidd, my love, my companion, my equally preposterously surnamed partner.

But most of all, I would like to thank my parents. My father passed on to me his love of education and inquiry; my mother gave me the passion and possession to make a life of those two things. (I also inherited her legs. Which—no offense, Dad—is a very lucky thing.) If I am proud of anything in this world, it is that they are proud of me.

Photo by Dylan Kidd

Elizabeth Little is a writer and editor living in New York City. Born in 1981, she first fell in love with languages at the tender age of five; at the time, however, language study took a back seat to her desire to be a member of Jem and the Holograms. She has since reconsidered.

In 2003, she graduated from Harvard University with a degree in political science and language citations in Mandarin and Classical Chinese. She has worked as a literary agent and as a writer and editor for the Let's Go guide to China, and her writing has appeared in the *New York Times*. Her free time is spent obsessively combing through conjugations and declensions, adding to her ever-expanding foreign-language library, and making increasingly futile attempts to master Hungarian.

This is her first book.